Pick-A-Pattern
APPLIQUÉ
& VARIATIONS

**Joan Sjuts
Waldman**

American Quilter's Society
P. O. Box 3290 • Paducah, KY 42002-3290
www.AQSquilt.com

Located in Paducah, Kentucky, the American Quilter's Society (AQS) is dedicated to promoting the accomplishments of today's quilters. Through its publications and events, AQS strives to honor today's quiltmakers and their work and to inspire future creativity and innovation in quiltmaking.

EDITOR: SHELLEY HAWKINS
GRAPHIC DESIGN: ELAINE WILSON
COVER DESIGN: MICHAEL BUCKINGHAM
PHOTOGRAPHY: CHARLES R. LYNCH

Library of Congress Cataloging-in-Publication Data
Waldman, Joan Sjuts.
    Pick-a-pattern applique & variations / Joan Waldman.
        p. cm.
Includes bibliographical references.
        ISBN 1-57432-803-4
1. Quilting--Patterns. 2. Appliqué--Patterns. I. Waldman, Joan.
II. Title.

TT835 .W333424   2002
746.46'041--dc21

                        2002152494

Additional copies of this book may be ordered from the American Quilter's Society, PO Box 3290, Paducah, KY 42002-3290, or online at www.AQSquilt.com.

Dedication

This book is dedicated to my husband, Harold, who patiently supports me in everything I attempt to do. Without him, I would not have had the opportunity to follow my dream.

It is also dedicated to my children, Cynthia, Randall, and Erick, who endured a mother with a needle in her hand during their growing years.

Acknowledgments

Thank you to the members of the Calico Quilt Club, who are always willing to try a new idea, and encourage me to push the limits just a little further.

A special thanks goes to my friends, Becky Keep, Sandy Kosch, Burnie Kratky, Sandi McMillan, Gloria Miller, Vivian Miller, Gail Parrott, Jackie Peterson, and Mary Weich, who helped stitch the quilts for this book. Without you, this project could not have been completed.

I would also like to thank Meredith Schroeder, without whom this book would not be possible, and the staff at AQS, who brought my designs to life: Michael Buckingham, Shelley Hawkins, Charles Lynch, Barbara Smith, and Elaine Wilson.

Contents

Introduction

A long-time interest in appliqué quilts led to my designing appliqué block patterns. Antique album quilts from the 1700s and 1800s inspired the patterns in this book. The album quilts ranged from simplistic folk art to intricate Baltimore Album designs. My designs are repeat patterns that are fairly easy to stitch by hand or machine.

For some of the blocks, I developed a method of drawing the pattern on the back of the background blocks, then basting, trimming, and needleturning the appliqué. Modern machine methods influenced additional design ideas.

The quilt settings presented in this book allow interchangeable blocks. This enables the use of different techniques when making the quilts. For example, the blocks in the REDWORK QUILT, page 60, feature traditional embroidery, while the blocks in the FAN FLOWERS STENCIL QUILT, page 34, were made with stencil paints.

Unlimited quilts can be made by changing the blocks in a setting and using different techniques to stitch, paint, stencil, or embroider the blocks. Hurried lifestyles demand methods that are fast, but ones that give pleasing results. An heirloom quilt can be made in a matter of weeks with these quick methods. Now, pick a technique, pick a setting, and pick a pattern to design a quilt that reflects your style.

Pick-A-Technique

The techniques in this section can be mixed or matched with any of the settings or patterns in this book. For each technique, you will need a heavy, permanent marker; tracing or lightweight paper; background fabric; and basic sewing supplies. Additional supplies are listed with the techniques.

The following are examples of patterns made with different techniques.

Pattern 42 (page 117), Technique 1 (page 10)

Pattern 42 (page 117), Technique 5 (page 18)

Pattern 3 (page 78), Technique 2 or 3 (page 15 or 16)

Pattern 3 (page 78), Technique 1 (page 14)

Pattern 10 (page 85), Technique 7 (page 20)

Pattern 10 (page 85), Technique 1 (page 13)

Pattern 26 (page 101), Technique 5 (page 18)

Pattern 26 (page 101), Technique 1 (page 10)

Pattern 48 (page 123), Technique 3 (page 16)

Pattern 48 (page 123), Technique 2 (page 15)

Pattern 40 (page 115), Technique 1 (page 10)

Pattern 40 (page 115), Technique 5 (page 18)

Appliqué

markers may be used for the pieces, such as green for leaves, red for flowers, yellow for centers, etc.

NEEDLETURN
Supplies

- Appliqué fabric
- Contrasting thread for basting
- Fine-line (.01), colored permanent markers
- Light box or other light source
- Thread to match appliqué

1 With a heavy, permanent marker, trace a full-size pattern on tracing or lightweight paper. Place the pattern, right side down, on a light box (Fig. 1–1), or tape it to a window. Lay the background fabric on top of the pattern, right side down.

2 Trace all pattern pieces ⅛" inside the shapes with a fine-line, colored permanent marker. By tracing ⅛" inside the pattern pieces, the lines will be covered when the appliqué is complete. Draw dashed lines where pieces overlap. Different color

3 To mark stem placement, turn the pattern and the background fabric to the right side. On the background fabric, draw a fine line through the center of each stem. To make the stems, cut bias strips ¾" wide, fold the bottom side to the halfway point, fold the top side over the bottom, and baste the stem through all three fabric layers (Fig. 1–2). This makes a ¼" stem. To vary the stem widths, cut the strips wider or narrower. For example, a strip cut ⅜" wide, when folded, would make a stem approximately ⅛" wide.

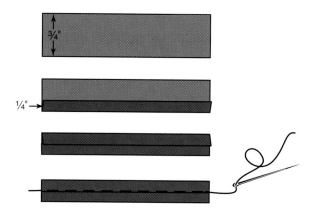

Fig. 1–2. Bias stem assembly.

Fig. 1–3. Blind stitch: Bring the needle up from under the appliqué and catch one or two threads of the appliqué. Slip the needle under the appliqué, directly under the first stitch, and through the background. Travel about ⅛" or less, bring the needle through the background, catch one or two threads, and repeat.

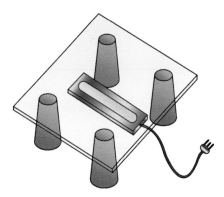

Fig. 1–1. Lightbox made from 18" plexiglass, edges smoothed; four water glasses (plastic); and undercounter light.

4 Stems are usually placed on the block first. Center the basted stem on top of the line drawn on the background. Using a blind stitch (Fig. 1–3, page 10), stitch the inside curve of the stem first. Then, stitch the outside curve in place. If the stem is straight, it makes no difference which side is stitched first.

5 Start flower appliqué with pieces that lie beneath others, such as a bud that is covered by a leaf. Lay the flower fabric, right side up, over the area where the piece will be stitched. Pin the pieces in place. Hold the block to a light to be sure the fabric covers the area to be stitched, plus at least ¼".

6 To secure appliqué fabric, turn the block to the back. Using highly contrasting thread, baste through the background and fabric on the traced line with running stitches (Fig. 1–4).

7 After basting, turn the block to the right side and trim the appliqué fabric, leaving a scant ¼" around all sides of the basting (Fig. 1–5).

8 To attach each piece, turn the edges of the piece under ⅛", halfway from the cut edge to the basting. If a piece has a place that needs clip-

ping, such as a dip in a flower petal, clip *halfway* to the basting, because only ⅛" is turned under when stitching (Fig. 1–6). Appliqué the pieces in place with a blind stitch and matching thread.

9 When all appliqué is complete, remove the basting stitches. The marked lines on the back of the block should now be ⅛" inside the appliqué stitching lines.

Fig. 1–5. Trim the appliqué fabric, leaving a scant ¼" turn-under allowance.

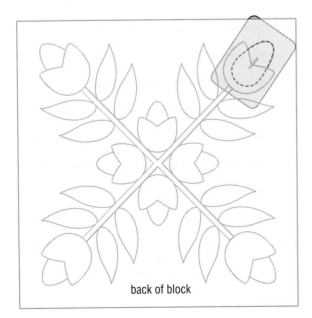

Fig. 1–4. Baste through the background and fabric.

Fig. 1–6. Where necessary, clip *halfway* to the basting.

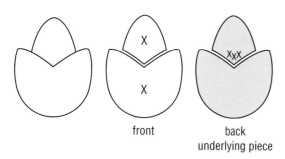

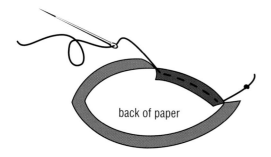

front   back
underlying piece

Fig. 1–7. Mark the pattern pieces.

back of paper

Fig. 1–8. Baste the turn-under allowance to the back of the paper.

Fig. 1–9. Allow about ⅛" extra fabric for underlying pieces.

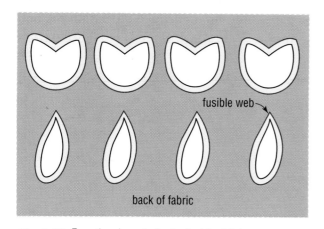

fusible web

back of fabric

Fig. 1–10. Fuse the pieces to the back of the fabric.

PAPER-BASTE
Supplies
  Appliqué fabric
  Contrasting thread for basting
  Thread to match appliqué
  Tweezers
  Typing-weight paper

1 With a heavy, permanent marker, trace a full-size pattern on tracing or lightweight paper.

2 Trace the pattern pieces to typing-weight paper. I recycle bulk-rate mailing paper for this. Cut out all pieces on the traced lines. Mark the right side of each pattern with an X. On the back of the patterns, mark edges that lie underneath others with several small x's (Fig. 1–7).

3 Pin the pattern pieces, right side down, to the back of the fabric. Cut the pieces out, adding a ⅜" turn-under allowance by eye.

4 Working the turn-under allowance to the back of the paper, baste it in place with contrasting thread. When basting, leave the knot at the end of the thread on top of the fabric appliqué piece (Fig. 1–8). There is no need to baste edges that lie underneath others. Clip curves as needed, leaving about two threads uncut at the edge of the paper.

5 Before placing the pieces on the background, appliqué the pieces into units with a blind stitch (see page 10). For example, if a flower has four pieces, appliqué them together. When the units are complete, position them on the background and appliqué in place. Leave approximately ½" unstitched for removing the paper.

6 Appliqué the remaining pieces. When ½" is left to be stitched on a piece, pull out the basting stitches and remove the paper pattern from the appliqué. Tweezers are helpful if you have trouble removing the paper. Finish stitching the piece to the background.

FREEZER PAPER/GLUE STICK
Supplies
- Appliqué fabric
- Freezer paper
- Thread to match appliqué
- Tweezers
- Washable glue stick

1 With a heavy, permanent marker, trace a full-size pattern on the paper side, not the shiny side, of the freezer paper. Cut out all the pieces on the traced sewing line.

2 Pin the freezer paper to the appliqué fabric, with the paper side to the back of the fabric (the shiny side should be showing). Allow at least ½" between pieces. Cut out the fabric, adding a scant ¼" seam allowance around each piece. Clip the inside curves almost to the paper. You may notch the outside edges to reduce bulk on the seam line.

3 With a washable glue stick, apply a line of glue at the edge of the freezer paper. Finger press the seam allowance over the freezer paper. Do not turn the edges that will lie under other pieces. Smooth the fabric edge as you press it over to keep bumps from forming at the fold. Use the handles of scissors or another hard object to smooth the seam. Allow the glue to dry.

4 Stitch pieces that lie on top of other pieces in place by hand or machine. Repeat this process, working in units, until all pieces are in place.

5 Center the appliqué on the background. Apply glue to the back of the units and place on the block. Allow the glue to dry, and hand or machine appliqué the design in place.

6 To remove the freezer paper, make a small cut in the background fabric behind the units. Use tweezers to pull the paper out. If the seam will not release, apply a damp washcloth over the area for a few seconds to soften the glue, then pull the paper out. Rinse the block and lay flat to dry. Press.

MACHINE FUSIBLE
Supplies
- Appliqué fabric
- Gray thread
- Light box or other light source
- Lightweight fusible web
- Matching, contrasting, or invisible thread
- Sewing machine

Machine appliqué can be done in many ways. I prefer using a lightweight fusible web and stitching around each piece with the machine. Some of the stitches I use include the blanket or buttonhole stitch; the blindhem stitch, if the stitch length and width can be adjusted; and a small zigzag stitch. The thread used in any of these stitches can either match or contrast with the appliqué. Invisible thread may be used as well. My personal preference is to use a darker shade of thread because it gives the illusion of an outline around the pieces. Bobbin thread is usually gray for this technique.

1 With a heavy, permanent marker, trace a full-size pattern on tracing or lightweight paper. Place the pattern, wrong side up, on a light box.

2 Lay the fusible web on top of the pattern, paper side up, and trace all the pieces onto the fusible web. Mark the edges where pattern pieces overlap with small x's. Allow about ⅛" extra fabric where one piece will lie beneath another. Designate this area with a dashed line on the paper side of fusible web (Fig. 1–9, page 12).

3 Rough cut the pieces from the fusible web, allowing some web to remain outside the drawn pattern. Fuse the pieces to the back of the fabric, following the manufacturer's directions (Fig. 1–10, page 12).

4 Cut out all of the pattern pieces. Allow a little extra fabric on pieces that lie beneath others.

5 Peel the paper from the back of the pieces and place them on the background block. Fuse the pieces in place. Appliqué around each piece with your desired stitch.

HAND FUSIBLE
Supplies

- Appliqué fabric
- Embroidery floss
- Light box or other light source
- Lightweight fusible web
- Matching or contrasting thread
- Small, sharp scissors

For this method, follow steps 1 and 2 in the machine fusible technique (page 13). Once traced, rough cut the pattern pieces from the fusible web, leaving about ¼" outside each drawn piece.

With small, sharp scissors, make windows in the fusible web by cutting a scant ¼" inside the drawn line of each piece. Fuse the pieces in place on the back of the fabric (Fig. 1–11). Then, cut out the pieces on the drawn line. Remove the paper and fuse the pieces in place on the block. Appliqué the pieces with a blanket or buttonhole stitch (Fig. 1–12). I prefer to use three strands of embroidery floss to do the stitching. Matching or contrasting threads can be used.

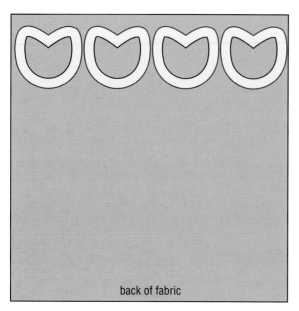

back of fabric

Fig. 1–11. Fuse the pieces in place on the back of the fabric.

(a)

(b)

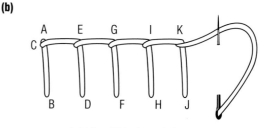

right-hand blanket stitch

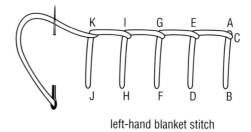

left-hand blanket stitch

Fig. 1–12. (a) Fuse the pieces in place on the block, and appliqué with the following stitch: (b) blanket (buttonhole) stitch.

Redwork

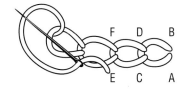

(a)

right-hand chain stitch

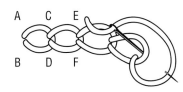

left-hand chain stitch

Supplies

Light box or other light source
Red embroidery floss
Water-soluble pen or silver pencil

1 With a heavy, permanent marker, trace a full-size pattern on tracing or lightweight paper. Place the pattern on a light box and lightly trace the design to the background block with a water-soluble pen or silver pencil.

2 Stitch the pattern with three strands of red embroidery floss, or use blue embroidery floss for Bluework. The most common stitches for this technique are the outline stitch and chain stitch (Fig. 1–13).

For traditional embroidery, any color of thread can be used for the patterns. If desired, colored pencils, fabric paints, or fabric crayons can be used to color in the patterns. After drying, these colors need to be heat set with an iron. If you are using fabric crayons, be sure to protect your ironing surface.

(b)

right-hand outline stitch

left-hand outline stitch

Fig. 1–13. (a) Chain stitch, (b) outline stitch.

3

Machine Redwork

Supplies

- Light box or other light source
- Red thread
- Sewing machine with darning foot
- Tear-away stabilizer
- Water-soluble pen or silver pencil
- Wooden screw-type embroidery hoop, 8–10"

1 Set your machine for free-form embroidery. Use a darning foot and drop the feed dogs. Thread the machine and bobbin with red thread.

2 With a heavy, permanent marker, trace a full-size pattern on tracing or lightweight paper. Lightly trace the pattern to the background block with a water-soluble pen or silver pencil.

3 Place the fabric in the embroidery hoop, with the pattern on the bottom of the hoop (Fig. 1–14). You may add a layer of tear-away stabilizer under the fabric to aid in stitching.

4 Begin by bringing the needle down through the fabric and pulling up the bobbin thread. Hold the threads while starting to stitch. Move the hoop back and forth along the pattern line. Sew about ½", go back over the stitch, then sew ahead about 1". Go back ½" again, then forward. Keep repeating the back-and-forth motion until there is a suitable thickness of thread. Three threads across a line are usually enough; however, sew back over the line as many times as you desire.

5 End the embroidery by stitching in place three or four times. Cut the threads and repeat the previous steps until all areas are stitched. Trim the threads.

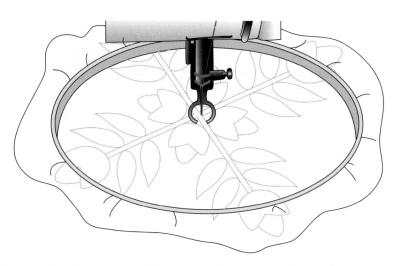

Fig. 1–14. Place the larger ring of the hoop beneath the fabric and the smaller ring on the top.

Watercolor Pencil

Supplies

Fabric medium
Fine-mist spray bottle
Hair dryer
Iron
Fabric marking pen (.01), black or colored
Spray sealer
Watercolor pencil set

There are several ways to paint blocks. Using watercolor pencils is one option. Watercolor should not be used on something that will be laundered frequently because it will fade after several washings.

1 With a heavy, permanent marker, trace a full-size pattern on tracing or lightweight paper. Trace the design onto the background fabric with a fabric marking pen. Heat set the outline with an iron.

2 Begin by painting the leaves and stems. Choose the darkest green or teal in your watercolor pencil set. Stroke around the outline of the leaves and stems. Press lightly on the pencil, building layers by gently stroking the color onto the fabric. Work the strokes in the direction that leaves grow, from tip to tip and not across the leaf. Gradually blend in lighter colors and finish with a little yellow or yellow-green over the center of the leaf for highlights. Color the flowers in the same manner (Fig. 1–15).

3 When you are finished painting the block, apply a fabric medium to keep the watercolor from fading. This can be found in the acrylic paint section of discount and craft stores. Mix one-third fabric medium to two-thirds water and pour the mixture in a fine-mist spray bottle. An empty eyeglass cleaner bottle usually makes a good spray bottle. Large droplets of the mixture should not fall on the fabric when sprayed.

4 Hold the spray bottle about 8"–10" from the fabric and lightly mist the colored design. Spray just enough to spread the colors. When you like the way it looks, use a hair dryer to quickly dry the surface of the fabric. Blow the air from the outside of the design toward the center to reduce bleeding. Some bleeding outside the lines is to be expected. That's the nature of watercolor – it runs.

5 Heat set the block with an iron. Add fine detail lines, such as the veins in leaves, with fabric marking pens.

6 Apply a coat of spray sealer. This helps keep the color from fading when the block is washed.

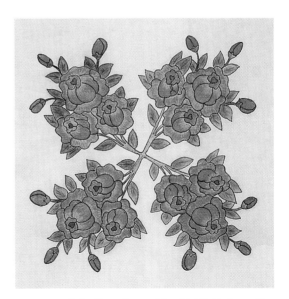

Fig. 1–15. Color the pattern, adding highlights for realism.

Stencil

Supplies

Contact paper, clear
Cutting mat
Freezer paper
Iron
Light box or other light source
Manila file folders
Paper towel
Safe-release masking tape
Sharp blade
Stencil brushes, preferably one for each color family
Stencil paint (creme)

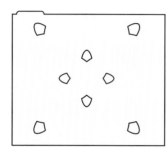

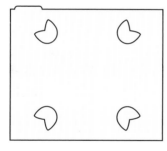

Fig. 1–16. Trace the pattern pieces for each color onto a separate file folder.

1 With a heavy, permanent marker, trace a full-size pattern on tracing or lightweight paper. Decide which parts of the pattern will be the same color. Indicate the colors on each pattern piece.

2 Lay the pattern on a light box. To make stencils, trace all the pattern pieces for one color onto a manila file folder with a permanent marker (Fig. 1–16). Always mark the top of each stencil to ensure proper orientation for placement. Using a new file folder for each color, trace the remaining pattern pieces.

3 Cover the traced side of the file folder with clear, contact paper. Be sure to have at least a couple of inches of contact paper around each traced piece.

4 Place the file folders on a cutting mat and, with a sharp blade, cut out all the patterns on the traced lines. If there is a piece that will fall out of the stencil when cut, leave a narrow bridge in the file folder to hold it in place (Fig. 1–17, page 19). Iron a square of freezer paper to the back of the fabric to be stenciled.

5 On the light box, lay the background fabric over the drawing from step 1. Position the cut-out stencil over the fabric and pattern. Tape the stencil to hold it in place. Move the block and stencil to a hard surface and tape in place. Use a

safe-release masking tape, which can be found in the paint supply section of department stores.

6 Using the desired colors of stencil paint, work a small amount of paint into the stencil brush. Rub the brush on a paper towel to distribute the paint evenly. Working from the outside edge of the stencil, lightly brush the paint onto the fabric. Do not work from the fabric toward the stencil because this will force the paint under the edges of the file folder. Brush with short strokes until the desired shading is accomplished. Another method of applying color is to tap the brush, straight up and down, on the fabric.

7 Repeat steps 5 and 6 for the remaining colors and stencils. Let the block dry for a few days, then heat set with an iron. Some stencil cremes have directions on the label for how long they take to dry. Wash the brushes with a brush cleaner or dishwashing liquid soap and water. Allow to them to air dry.

Acrylic Paint

Supplies
- Embroidery floss
- Light box or other light source
- Fabric marking pen (.01)
- Transparent acrylic paints

1 With a heavy, permanent marker, trace a full-size pattern on tracing or lightweight paper. Place the pattern on a light box and lay the background block on top of the pattern. Lightly trace the pattern to the block with a fabric marking pen. The pen lines, which will show through the transparent paint, can be left as detailing when the block is complete.

2 Using transparent acrylic paints, paint the block as desired. Let the paint dry, then heat set. Stitch the outlines by hand with embroidery floss or by machine, following the technique described in Machine Redwork, page 16.

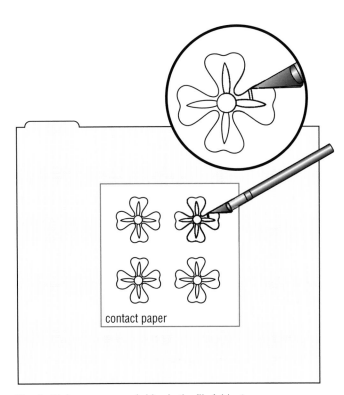

Fig. 1–17. Leave a narrow bridge in the file folder to hold pieces in place.

Trapunto

Supplies

- Cotton batting or extra-loft poly batting
- Light box or other light source
- Regular sewing thread
- Sewing machine with darning foot
- Small, blunt-end scissors
- Washable marker
- Water-soluble thread

1 With a heavy, permanent marker, trace a full-size pattern on tracing or lightweight paper. Place the pattern on a light box and trace it on the background block with a washable marker.

2 Place two layers of cotton batting, or one layer of extra-loft poly batting, behind the traced block. Thread your machine with water-soluble thread on the top and regular white sewing thread in the bobbin. Set the machine for free-form quilting. Drop the feed dogs and use a darning foot.

3 Stitch around the entire outline of the pattern, being sure that the stitching makes a complete circle around the design. Do not stitch any details at this time, just outline the pattern (Fig. 1–18).

4 Using small, blunt-end scissors, trim away excess batting outside the outline stitching. Be careful not to cut the background block. When finished, layer the block or quilt with backing and batting. Pin the layers together and re-stitch all lines, using regular sewing thread on top and in the bobbin.

5 After the outline is finished, a second row of stitching may be added two or three threads outside the first, then add any details that you desire. Quilt the background in straight lines or stipple quilt. Soak the block in cold water to remove the marker and dissolve the water-soluble thread.

Fig. 1–18. Stitch the outline of the pattern through the block and the batting.

Pick-A-Setting

Fifteen different settings, using a variety of patterns from the following Pick-A-Pattern section and from one to 13 blocks in various arrangements, make up this section. Complete the blocks, using the technique or your choice, before assembly.

The yardage given with the setting indicates how much fabric is required for the background blocks, borders, backing, and binding.

Quilt assembly instructions are given with each setting. Please refer to "Finishing Your Quilt," page 127, for border, machine quilting, and binding instructions.

LOVELY LEAVES

Quilt size: 45" x 45"
Finished block size: 14"

Pattern 25, Crossed Leaves, page 100, was used
in this quilt made by the author.

YARDAGE

Yardage is based on a 40"–45" WOF (width of fabric).

⅝ yard red fabric

1⅞ yards white fabric

49" x 49" batting

2⅞ yards backing

⅜ yard binding

CUTTING

Blocks:

Four 16" white squares, trimmed to 14½"
after the blocks are appliquéd

Sashing:

1 red square 3½"

4 red strips 1½" x 14½"

4 red strips 1½" x 15½"

4 white strips 3½" x 15½"

Borders:

2 red strips 1½" x 33½" for inner top and
bottom borders

2 red strips 1½" x 35½" for inner
side borders

4 white strips 5½" x 35½" for outer borders

4 red squares 5½" for corners

Backing:

49" x 49"

Binding:

5 strips 2¼" x WOF"

ASSEMBLY

Use a ¼" seam allowance for piecing.

❖ Complete four blocks. Sew the 1½" red sashing strips to adjacent sides of each appliquéd block as shown (Fig. 2–1).

❖ Join two blocks vertically with a 3½" x 15½" white strip. Repeat with the other two blocks and a white strip. Sew the 3½" red square between the last two 3½" x 15½" white strips to make the center sashing. Sew the two block rows to the center sashing (Fig. 2–2, page 24).

❖ Sew the 1½" x 33½" red strips to the top and bottom of the assembled rows. Then, sew the 1½" x 35½" red strips to the sides to complete the inner border.

❖ Add two of the 5½" white border strips to sides of the quilt. Sew a 5½" red square on each end of the remaining white border strips. Attach the assembled outer borders to the top and bottom of the quilt.

❖ Layer the batting between the backing and quilt top. Quilt as desired, bind, and place a label on your quilt

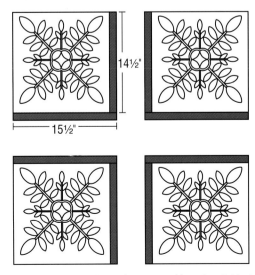

Fig. 2–1. Sew the red sashing strips to two sides of each block.

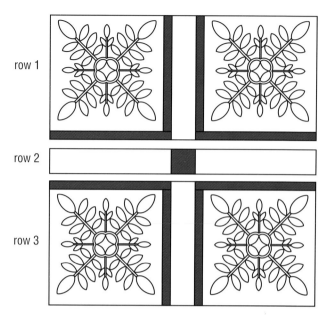

row 1

row 2

row 3

Fig. 2–2. Make three rows.

Quilt assembly.

GAIL'S TULIP CIRCLE

Quilt size: 62" x 62"
Finished block size: 14"

Pattern 9, Tulip Circle, page 84, was used in this quilt
made by Gail Parrott, Council Bluffs, Iowa.

YARDAGE

Yardage is based on a 40"–45" WOF (width of fabric).

4⅛ yards white fabric

¾ yard green fabric for bias vines

1⅜ yards solid or assorted fabrics for points
(fabrics from appliqué can be used)

66" x 66" batting

3⅞ yards backing

⅝ yard binding, if you choose to
turn outer points inward

CUTTING

Cut borders first, parallel to the selvage.

Borders:

2 white strips 10½" x 44" for top and bottom
borders

2 white strips 10½" x 64" for side borders

Blocks:

9 white squares 16", trimmed to 14½" after
the blocks are appliquéd

Prairie Points:

280 assorted squares 2½"

Border vine:

Green bias strips ¾" to equal approximately
280"

Backing:

66" x 66"

ASSEMBLY

Use a ¼" seam allowance for piecing.

❉ Make the prairie points for the quilt by folding the 2½" squares in half diagonally. Press, then fold the squares diagonally again so that all raw edges are on one side. Press again (Fig. 2–3).

❉ Complete nine blocks. Join the blocks into three rows of three blocks. Sew the rows together.

❉ To sew the points to the quilt center, match the raw edges of the points to the raw edges of the assembled blocks. Pin 25 points along each side of the quilt center. The points can be overlapped to fit. Baste the points in place with a scant ¼" seam allowance (Fig. 2–4, page 27).

❉ Sew the top and bottom borders to the assembled blocks. Then, sew the side borders to the quilt. Press the points out toward the border. For the points on the outer edge of the quilt, pin 45 points along the edge of each border and baste as before. Press the points outward.

❉ For the border vine, join the ¾" strips into one long strip. Fold the strip as shown in Fig. 1–2, page 10, and baste. Pin the bias strip in place, following the directions in "Designing your own border," page 128. Add appliqué on the borders as desired by using flowers and leaves from the blocks chosen for the quilt.

❉ Layer the batting between the backing and quilt top. Turn the backing under ¼" and stitch to the back of the points. Quilt as desired, and place a label on your quilt.

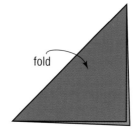
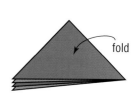

Fig. 2–3. Fold the 2½" squares to make the prairie points.

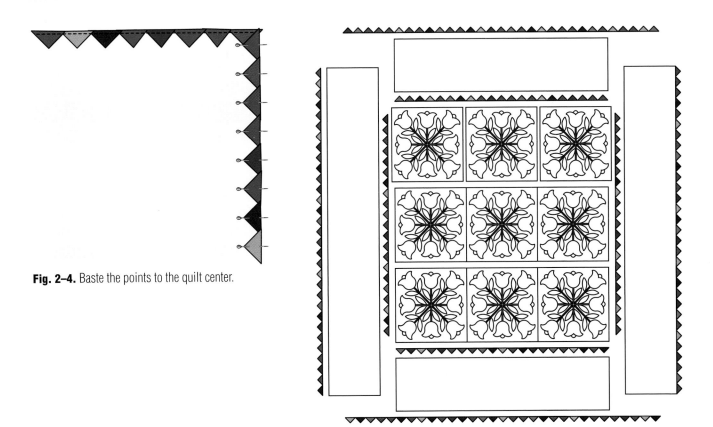

Fig. 2–4. Baste the points to the quilt center.

Quilt assembly.

Border vine placement.

3

LOOKS LIKE CHERRIES TO ME

Quilt size: 62" x 62"
Finished block size: 14"

Pattern 15, Looks Like Cherries to Me, page 90, was used in this quilt made by Becky Keep, Columbus, Nebraska.

YARDAGE

Yardage is based on a 40"–45" WOF (width of fabric).

 4⅛ yards white fabric

 1⅛ yards red fabric

 1 yard green fabric

 66" x 66" batting

 3⅞ yards backing

 ⅝ yard binding

CUTTING

Cut borders first, parallel to the selvage.

Borders and sashing:

 2 white strips 2½" x 52" for inner
  side borders

 2 white strips 2½" x 56" for inner top and
  bottom borders

 12 red strips 2½" x WOF

 13 green strips 2½" x WOF

 1 red strip 4½" x WOF

Blocks:

 9 white squares 16", trimmed to 14½" after
  the blocks are appliquéd

Backing:

 66" x 66"

Binding:

 7 strips 2½" x WOF

ASSEMBLY

Use a ¼" seam allowance for piecing.

❖ Complete nine blocks. For the sashing and borders, make three strip-sets consisting of four red strips and three green strips as shown. Cut the strips-sets into twenty-four 2½" segments and twelve 4½" segments (Fig. 2–5).

❖ From the four remaining 2½" green strips, cut sixteen 2½" squares and twenty 4½" strips. From the one 4½" red strip, cut four 2½" strips and four 4½" squares. Refer to Fig. 2–6 and join the strip-set segments and 2½" green squares to form four sashing rows. Then, join the strip-set segments and blocks to form three block rows.

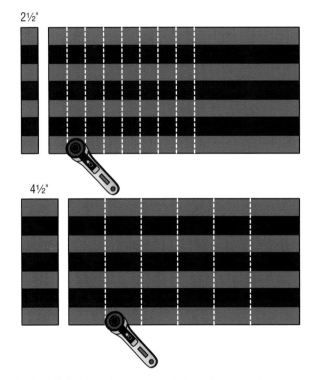

2½"

4½"

Fig. 2–5. Cut 2½" and 4½" segments from the strip-sets.

sashing row

block row

Fig. 2–6. Assemble four sashing rows and three block rows.

❖ Sew the assembled rows together to form the quilt center. Add the white border strips to the sides of the quilt, then to the top and bottom, trimming each strip to size after stitching.

❖ Refer to Fig. 2–7 and assemble four outer borders, adding the 2½" x 4½" segments as shown. Attach the borders to the sides of the quilt. Add two 4½" red squares to each side of the top and bottom border strips, and add the borders to the quilt.

❖ Layer the batting between the backing and quilt top. Quilt as desired, bind, and place a label on your quilt.

2½"

4½"

Fig. 2–7. Assemble four outer borders.

Quilt assembly.

GRAPES

Quilt size: 34" x 34"
Finished block size: 14"

Pattern 42, Grape Ring, page 117, was used in this quilt
made by Burnie Kratky, Columbus, Nebraska.

YARDAGE

Yardage is based on a 40"–45" WOF (width of fabric).

1 yard total of assorted tone-on-tone
   cream fabrics
½ yard green fabric
38" x 38" batting
1⅛ yards backing
⅜ yard binding

CUTTING
Block:

4 cream squares 6⅞", cut in half diagonally
4 cream rectangles 2½" x 6½"
1 square 2½"

Borders:

2 green strips 2½" x 14½" for inner side borders
2 green strips 2½" x 18½" for inner top and
   bottom borders
16 assorted cream squares 6⅞", cut in half
   diagonally
2 green strips 2½" x 30½" for outer
   side borders
2 green strips 2½" x 34½" for outer top and
   bottom borders

Backing:

38" x 38"

Binding:

4 strips 2½" x WOF

ASSEMBLY
Use a ¼" seam allowance for piecing.

❖ The background for this block is pieced. Assemble the pieces cut for the background block and sew them together as shown (Fig. 2–8).

❖ Appliqué your chosen pattern on the background block. For the grapes on this sample quilt, 2¼" circles were used. The raw edges were turned under ¼" and basted around the edge of the circle. Thread was pulled tight and knotted securely to make a yo-yo. The leaves and stems are appliquéd on the block before the yo-yos.

❖ Sew the 2½" x 14½" green strips to the sides of block. Then sew the 2½" x 18½" green strips to the top and bottom. Mix the assorted cream triangles cut for the border and sew two together on the long sides to form 16 squares.

❖ Sew three of the cream squares together and add to the side of the quilt. Repeat this step for the other side. Sew five of the cream squares together to form the top and bottom borders and attach to the quilt. Add the outer 2½" x 30½" strips to sides of quilt, then sew the 2½" x 34½" strips to the top and bottom to complete the quilt top.

❖ Layer the batting between the backing and quilt top. Quilt as desired. In this quilt, some of the border squares are quilted in straight lines ½" and 1" apart. Several squares contain a motif (see the pattern on page 33). Bind and place a label on your quilt.

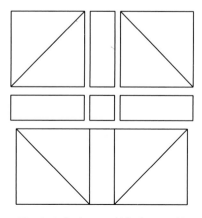

Fig. 2–8. Background block assembly.

Quilt assembly.

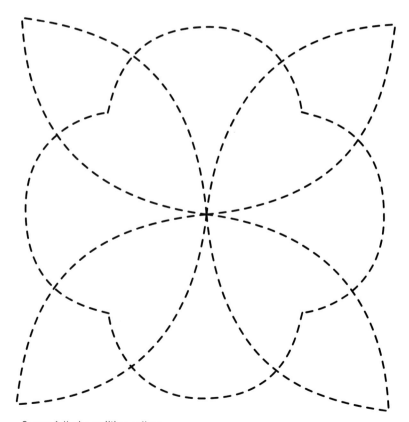

GRAPES full-size quilting pattern.

FAN FLOWERS STENCIL QUILT

Quilt size: 74" x 90"
Finished block size: 14"

Pattern 26, Crossed Fan Flowers, page 101, was used in this quilt made by the author.

YARDAGE

Yardage is based on a 40"–45" WOF (width of fabric).

5 yards white fabric

2⅝ yards pink fabric

78" x 94" batting

5⅜ yards backing

⅝ yard binding

CUTTING

Cut borders first, parallel to the selvage.

Borders:

2 white strips 10½" x 68" for inner side borders

2 white strips 10½" x 72" for inner top and bottom borders

2 pink strips 2½" x 88" for outer side borders

2 pink strips 2½" x 76" for outer top and bottom borders

Blocks:

12 white squares 15", trimmed to 14½" after the blocks are stenciled

Sashing:

8 pink strips 2½" x 14½"

5 pink strips 2½" x 46½"

2 pink strips 2½" x 66½"

Backing:

78" x 94"

Binding:

9 strips 2¼" x WOF

ASSEMBLY

Use a ¼" seam allowance for piecing.

❖ Choose a pattern and refer to stencil instructions, page 18, to make 12 blocks. The colors of the Fan Flowers block are numbered in Fig. 2–9 for stenciling.

❖ Refer to the quilt assembly diagram, page 36, and join two 2½" x 14½" sashing strips between three blocks. Make four of these rows. Add a 2½" x 46½" strip between the rows, and then to the top and bottom of the pieced rows.

Sew a 2½" x 66½" strip to each side of the pieced rows.

❖ Sew the white 10½" border strips to the sides, and then to the top and bottom of the quilt top, trimming each strip to size after stitching. Add the outer pink 2½" border strips in the same manner.

❖ Refer to the patterns on pages 37–40 and add border stenciling. The patterns contain numbers for color placement. Layer the batting between the backing and quilt top. Quilt as desired, bind, and place a label on your quilt.

Fig. 2–9. Color guide for stenciling.

Quilt assembly.

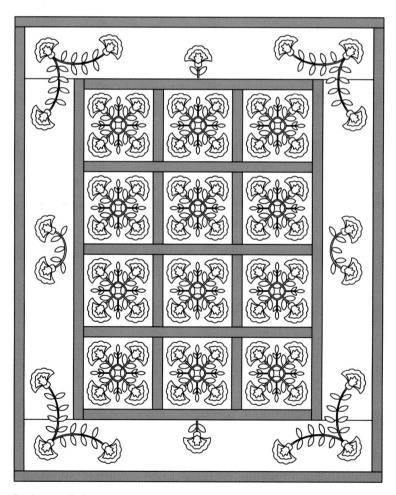

Border stencil placement.

FAN FLOWERS STENCIL QUILT
side border stencil

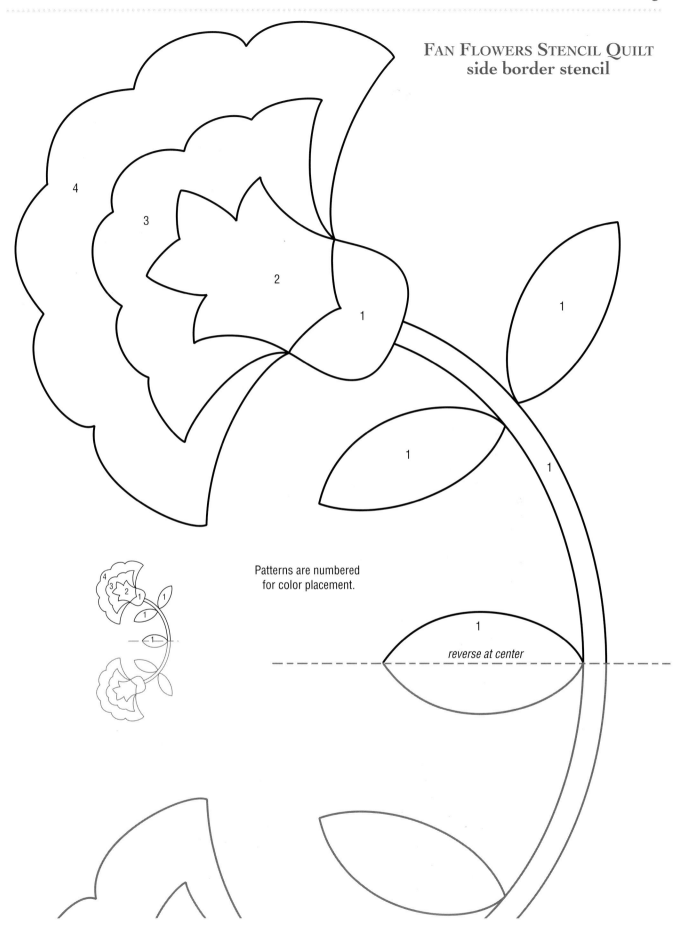

Patterns are numbered
for color placement.

reverse at center

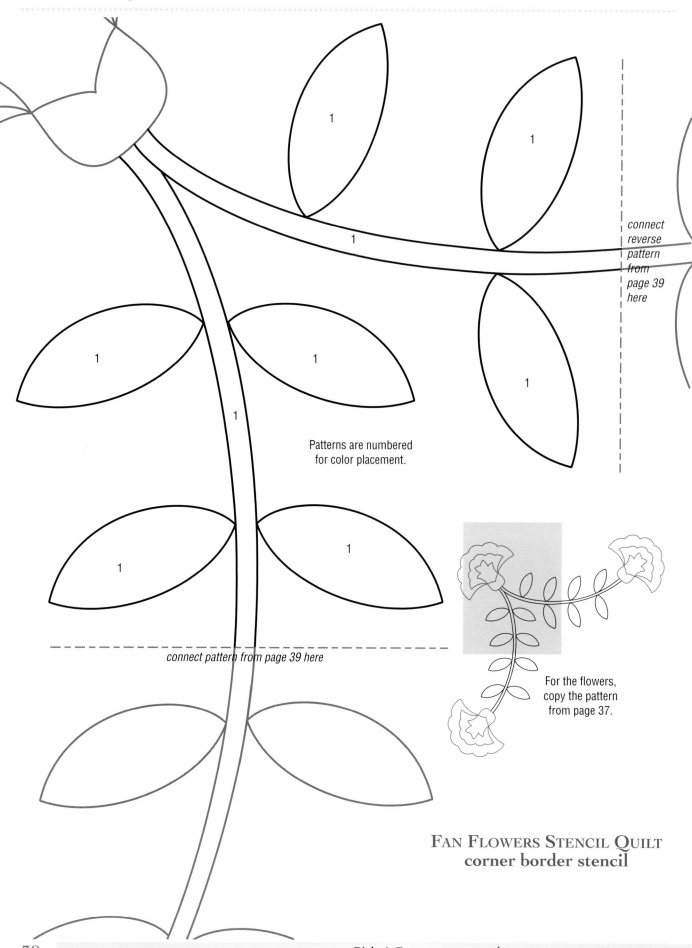

1

1

1

1

1

1

connect
reverse
pattern
from
page 39
here

1

Patterns are numbered
for color placement.

1

1

For the flowers,
copy the pattern
from page 37.

connect pattern from page 39 here

FAN FLOWERS STENCIL QUILT
corner border stencil

Pick-A-Pattern APPLIQUÉ & VARIATIONS – *Joan Waldman*

connect here

1

1

1

1

1

1

Patterns are numbered
for color placement.

FAN FLOWERS STENCIL QUILT
corner border stencil

FAN FLOWERS STENCIL QUILT
top and bottom border stencil

Patterns are numbered
for color placement.

ART DECO IRIS

Quilt size: 86" x 86"
Finished block size: 14"

Pattern 2, Iris, page 77, was used in this quilt made by the author.

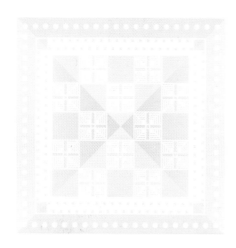

YARDAGE
Yardage is based on a 40"–45" WOF (width of fabric).

4¾ yards white fabric

1⅛ yards black fabric

⅜ yard light fabric

⅞ yard medium-light fabric

1 yard medium-dark fabric

1¼ yards dark fabric

90" x 90" batting

7⅞ yards backing

¾ yard binding

CUTTING:
Cut borders strips first.

Borders:

8 black strips 2½" x WOF" for inner borders

10 white strips 2½" x WOF for outer borders

3 medium-light strips 4½" x WOF for outer borders

3 medium-dark strips 4½" x WOF for outer borders

4 dark strips 4½" x WOF for outer borders

4 black squares 6½" for corners

Blocks:

13 white squares 16", trimmed to 14½" after the blocks are appliqued

Log Cabin blocks:

60 black squares 2½"

48 white strips 2½" x 6½"

8 light strips 1½" x WOF

10 medium-light strips 1½" x WOF

13 medium-dark strips 1½" x WOF

15 dark strips 1½" x WOF

Backing:

90" x 90"

Binding:

9 strips 2¼" x WOF

ASSEMBLY
Use a ¼" seam allowance for piecing.

❖ Complete 13 appliqué blocks. Construct 48 Log Cabin units as follows: On one side of a 2½" black square, sew a light 1½" strip. Trim the strip even with the square. Then, sew the light strip to the adjoining side of the black square, and trim. Continue adding the medium-light, medium-dark, and dark strips in the same manner to complete each Log Cabin unit (Fig. 2–10).

❖ Assemble the Log Cabin units into 12 blocks as follows: Sew a 2½" x 6½" white strip between two Log Cabin blocks. Repeat. Sew a 2½" black square between two 2½" x 6½" white strips. Sew the three pieced rows together (Fig. 2–11, page 43). Make 12 pieced blocks.

❖ Refer to the quilt assembly diagram and join the appliquéd and pieced blocks. Sew the 2½" black

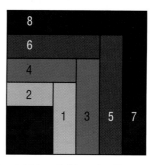

Fig. 2–10. Construct 48 Log Cabin units. Numbers 1 and 2 contain light strips, 3 and 4 contain medium-light strips, 5 and 6 contain medium-dark strips, and 7 and 8 contain dark strips.

inner border strips together, end to end. Add the borders to the sides of the quilt, then to the top and bottom, trimming each strip to size after stitching.

❖ To construct the outer borders, sew a white 2½" strip to each of the medium-light, medium-dark, and dark 4½" strips to make a total of 10 strip-sets. Press the seam allowance toward the dark fabric. From the strip-sets, cut 2½" segments (Fig. 2–12).

❖ Arrange the 2½" x 6½" segments randomly, alternating the direction of the dark patch with each strip. Sew 37 segments together to form one border. Repeat for the other three sides. Sew the borders to the sides of the quilt. Add a 6½" black square to each side of the remaining two borders and attach to the top and bottom of the quilt.

❖ Layer the batting between the backing and quilt top. Quilt as desired, bind, and place a label on your quilt.

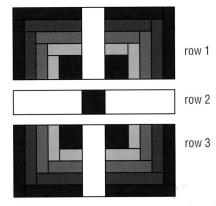

row 1

row 2

row 3

Fig. 2–11. Block assembly.

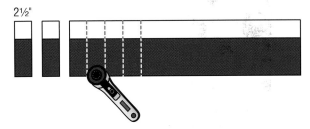

2½"

Fig. 2–12. Cut the strip-sets into 2½" segments.

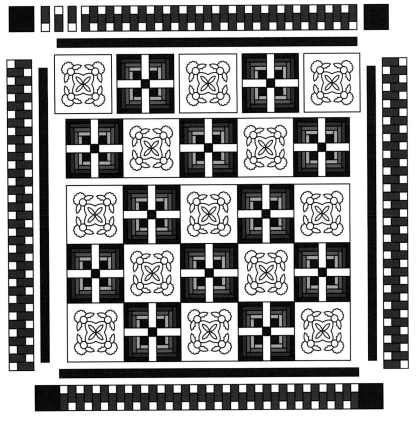

Quilt assembly.

SPINNING TULIPS

Quilt size: 22" x 22"
Finished block size: 14"

Pattern 3, Spinning Tulips 1, page 78, was used in this quilt made by the author. You will need embroidery floss if you choose to blanket-stitch appliqué.

YARDAGE

Yardage is based on a 40"–45" WOF (width of fabric).

⅞ yard white fabric

½ yard blue fabric

26" x 26" batting

¾ yard backing

¼ yard binding

CUTTING

Blocks:

1 white square 16", trimmed to 14½" after the block is appliquéd

Borders:

2 white strips 4½" x 14½" for top and bottom borders

2 white strips 4½" x 22½" for side borders

Prairie Points:

72 blue squares 2½"

Backing:

26" x 26"

Binding:

3 strips 2¼" x WOF

ASSEMBLY

Use a ¼" seam allowance for piecing, unless otherwise noted.

❖ Complete one block. Make the prairie points for the borders by folding the 2½" squares in half diagonally. Press, then fold the square diagonally again so that all raw edges are on one side (Fig. 2–13). Press again.

❖ Pin seven points along each side of the block. The points can be overlapped to fit. Baste the points in place with a scant ¼" seam. Lay the top and bottom borders over the points and sew them to the block (Fig. 2–14, page 46). Then, sew the side borders to the block. Press the points in the direction desired.

❖ Appliqué a design in the border. See page 47 for the Spinning Tulips design.

❖ Pin 11 points to each border edge. The points can be overlapped to fit. Baste the points in place about ⅛" from the raw edges.

❖ Layer the batting between the backing and quilt top. If you want the points to face inward, apply binding to the edge of the quilt as usual. If you want the points to face outward, turn the seam of the points under and press. Bring the backing to the edge of the points and turn under ¼". Sew the backing to the points with a blind stitch. Binding is eliminated if the points face outward. Quilt as desired, and place a label on your quilt.

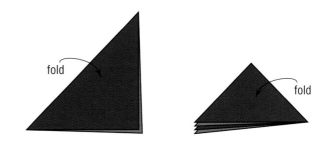

Fig. 2–13. Fold the 2½" squares to make the prairie points.

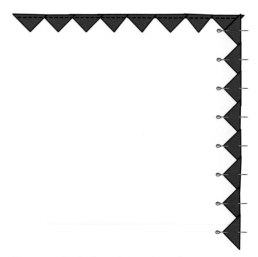

Fig. 2–14. Baste the points to the quilt center.

Quilt assembly.

SPINNING TULIPS
full-size
border appliqué pattern

Border appliqué placement.

COMPASS FLOWER TRAPUNTO
Quilt size: 23½" x 23½"
Finished block size: 14"

Pattern 10, Compass Flower, page 85, was used in this quilt made by the author.

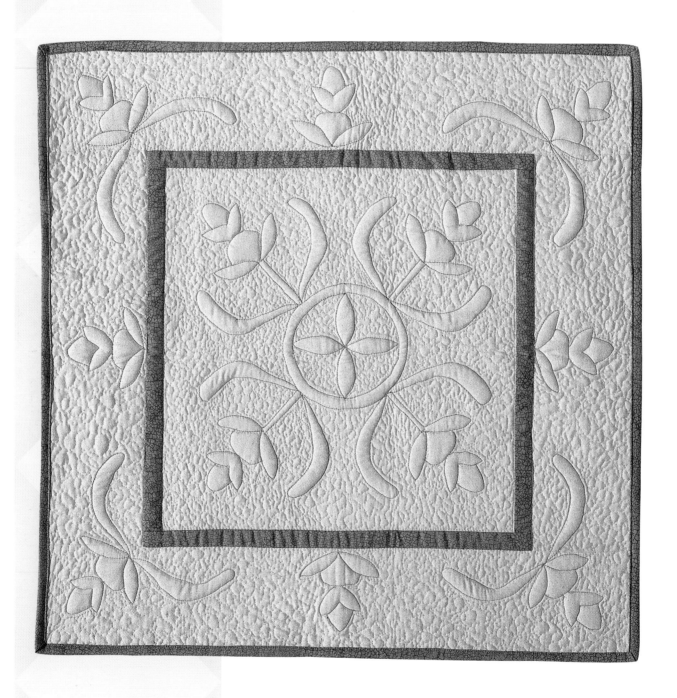

YARDAGE

Yardage is based on a 40"–45" WOF (width of fabric).

⅞ yard cream fabric

⅛ yard green fabric

27½" x 27½" high-loft polyester batting

Two 27½" x 27½" cotton battings

⅞ yard backing

⅜ yard binding

CUTTING

Block:

1 cream square 14½"

Borders:

2 green strips 1¼" x 14½" for inner
side borders

2 green strips 1¼" x 16" for inner top
and bottom borders

2 cream strips 4½" x 16" for outer
side borders

2 cream strips 4½" x 24" for outer top
and bottom borders

Backing:

27½" x 27½"

Binding:

3 strips 2¼" x WOF

ASSEMBLY

Use a ¼" seam allowance for piecing.

❧ Sew the inner side borders to the white block, then sew the top and bottom inner borders. Add the outer borders in the same manner. Trace your desired pattern on the block with a water-soluble marker or a silver quilter's pencil. For the border design, trace elements from the pattern. See page 50 for the Compass Flower border design.

❧ Quilt the assembled top by following the directions for trapunto, page 20, and machine quilting, page 130. The background of the quilt is stipple quilted with invisible thread on top and bobbin/lingerie thread on bottom of the machine.

❧ Bind and place a label on your quilt.

Quilt assembly.

Border pattern placement.

COMPASS FLOWER TRAPUNTO
full-size border pattern

AROUND TULIP TIME

Quilt size: 27" x 27"
Finished block size: 14"

Pattern 18, Tulip Time 1, page 93, was used in this quilt made by the author.
You will need embroidery floss if you choose to blanket-stitch appliqué.

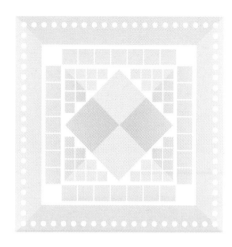

YARDAGE
Yardage is based on a 40"–45" WOF (width of fabric).

 ½ yard white fabric
 ⅛ yard light fabric
 ¼ yard medium-light fabric
 ¼ yard medium fabric
 ¼ yard medium-dark fabric
 ⅝ yard dark fabric
 31" x 31" batting
 1 yard backing
 ⅜ yard binding

CUTTING
Block:

 1 white square 16", trimmed to 14½" after the
  block is appliquéd

Setting triangles:

 20 dark squares 2½"
 16 medium-dark squares 2½"
 12 medium squares 2½"
 8 medium-light squares 2½"
 4 light squares 2½"

Borders:

 2 dark strips 1" x 22" for inner side borders
 2 dark strips 1" x 24" for inner top and
  bottom borders
 4 dark squares 3½" for corners
 8 medium-dark squares 3½" for outer borders
 8 mediums squares 3½" for outer borders

 8 medium-light squares 3½" for outer borders
 4 light squares 3½" for outer borders

Backing:

 31" x 31"

Binding:

 4 strips 2¼" x WOF

ASSEMBLY
Use a ¼" seam allowance for piecing.

❖ Complete one block. Refer to Fig. 2–15, page 53, to make four corner sections of the quilt in rows. Each section contains the following 2½" squares: one light, two medium-light, three medium, four medium-dark, and five dark. Trim the dark squares in half diagonally, leaving a ¼" seam allowance beyond the points (Fig. 2–16, page 53).

❖ Sew a corner section to one side of the block, then sew another section to the opposite side of the block. Press the seams toward the corners. Add corner sections to the remaining two sides of the block. Sew the two inner side borders to the quilt, then sew the inner top and bottom borders.

❖ Refer to Fig. 2–17, page 53, and make four outer borders. Each border contains the following 3½" squares: one light, two medium-light, two medium, and two medium-dark.

❖ Attach a border to the sides of the quilt. Sew a dark 3½" square to each end of the remaining two borders and attach them to the top and bottom of the quilt.

❖ Layer the batting between the backing and quilt top. Quilt as desired, bind, and place a label on your quilt.

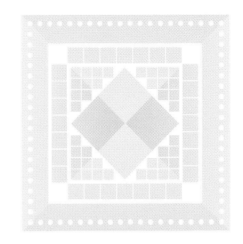

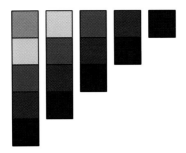

Fig. 2–15. Piece the 2½" squares to form the corner sections.

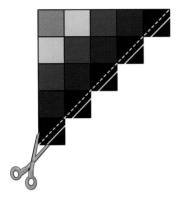

Fig. 2–16. Trim the dark squares, leaving a ¼" seam allowance.

Fig. 2–17. Make four outer borders.

Quilt assembly.

CROSSROADS

Quilt size: 90" x 90"
Finished block size: 14"

The following patterns were used in this quilt: 31, Crossed Flowers, page 106; 32, Peony Ring, page 107; 33, Love Apple Ring, page 108; 34, Dogwood Ring, page 109; 35, Rose Ring, page 110; 36, Tulip Ring, page 111; 37, Clematis Ring, page 112; 38, Sunflower Ring, page 113; 39, Cockscomb Ring, page 114; 40, Candle Flower Ring, page 115; 41, Cone Flower Ring, page 116; 42, Grape Ring, page 117; and 43, Poppy Ring, page 118. The quilt was made by Sandi McMillan, Albion, Nebraska.

Pick-A-Pattern APPLIQUÉ & VARIATIONS – Joan Waldman

YARDAGE

Yardage is based on a 40"–45" WOF (width of fabric).

8⅜ yards maroon fabric

12 assorted fat quarters of light fabric for
Irish Chain and floral appliqué

1¾ yards green fabric for border appliqué

1¾ yards gold fabric for border appliqué

94" x 94" batting

8¼ yards backing

⅞ yard binding

CUTTING

Cut borders first, parallel to the selvage.

Borders:

4 maroon strips 10½" x 92½"

Appliqué blocks:

13 maroon squares 16", trimmed to 14½" after
the blocks are appliquéd

Irish Chain blocks:

156 assorted light squares 2½"

72 maroon squares 2½"

48 maroon strips 2½" x 4½"

48 maroon strips 2½" x 6½"

24 maroon strips 2½" x 10½"

Backing:

94" x 94"

Binding:

10 strips 2¼" x WOF

ASSEMBLY

Use a ¼" seam allowance for piecing.

❖ Make 13 appliqué blocks. Make 12 Irish Chain blocks as shown in Fig. 2–18. Each block contains 13 assorted 2½" light squares and the following maroon pieces: six 2½" squares, four 2½" x 4½" strips, four 2½" x 6½" strips, and two 2½" x 10½" strips.

❖ Refer to the quilt assembly diagram, page 56, and sew five rows of five blocks as shown, alternating appliqué and Irish Chain blocks. Attach the maroon borders to the quilt top and miter the corners. Add an appliqué design to the border. See page 57 for the Crossroads border design.

❖ Layer the batting between the backing and quilt top. Quilt as desired, bind, and place a label on your quilt.

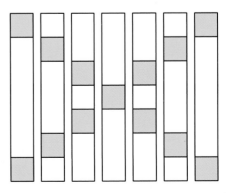

Fig. 2–18. Make 12 Irish Chain blocks.

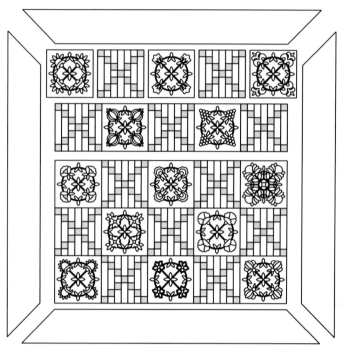

Quilt assembly.

Add border appliqué.

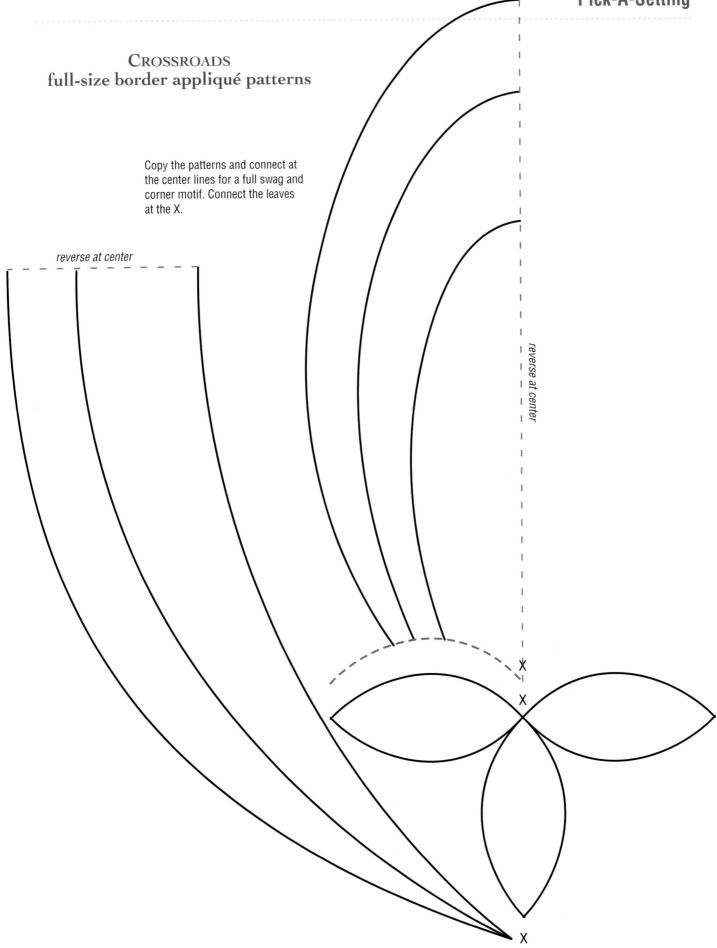

CROSSROADS
full-size border appliqué patterns

Copy the patterns and connect at
the center lines for a full swag and
corner motif. Connect the leaves
at the X.

reverse at center

reverse at center

11

LOG CABIN TABLE TOPPER

Quilt size: 22" x 22"

Pattern 19, Tulip Time 2, page 94, was used in this quilt
made by Sandra K. Kosch, Shelby, Nebraska.

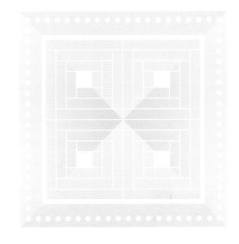

YARDAGE

Yardage is based on a 40"–45" WOF (width of fabric).

⅜ yard assorted light fabrics

⅛ yard medium fabric

½ yard assorted dark fabrics

26" x 26" batting

¾ yard backing

⅜ yard binding

CUTTING

Log Cabin blocks:

4 medium squares 2½"

4 light strips 2" wide by each of the following lengths: 2½", 4", 5½", 7", 8½", and 10"

4 dark strips 2" wide by each of the following lengths: 4" x 5½", 7", 8½", 10", and 11½"

Backing:

26" x 26"

Binding:

3 strips 2¼" x WOF

ASSEMBLY

Use a ¼" seam allowance for piecing.

❖ Make four Log Cabin blocks as shown in Fig. 2–19, sewing the light and dark strips to the 2½" medium square counter-clockwise in the order indicated.

❖ Sew the four blocks together, placing the light portions of the blocks toward the center. Appliqué your desired pattern over the pieced Log Cabin blocks.

❖ Layer the batting between the backing and quilt top. Quilt as desired, bind, and place a label on your quilt.

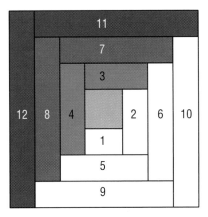

Fig. 2–19. Log Cabin assembly. Numbers 1, 2, 5, 6, 9, and 10 contain light strips, and numbers 3, 4, 7, 8, 11, and 12 contain dark strips.

Quilt assembly.

REDWORK QUILT

Quilt size: 60½" x 60½"
Finished block size: 14"

The following patterns were used in this quilt: 46, Cosmos, page 121; 47, Roses, page 122; 48, Gaillardia, page 123; 49, Nasturtiums, page 124; and 50, Poinsettia, page 125. The quilt was made by the author. You will need 25 skeins of red embroidery floss, split into three strands before stitching the blocks and borders.

YARDAGE
Yardage is based on a 40"–45" WOF (width of fabric).

2⅜ yards white fabric

2½ yards red fabric

65" x 65" batting

3⅝ yards backing

⅝ yard binding

CUTTING
Cut fabric in the order indicated.
Setting triangles:

2 red strips 3¾" x WOF for side triangles

2 white strips 2½" x WOF for side triangles

2 red strips 5¼" x WOF for side triangles

2 red squares 10⅞", cut in half diagonally, for corners

Borders:

2 red strips 1½" x 42" or inner side borders

2 red strips 1½" x 44" for inner top and bottom borders

2 white strips 6" x 44" for middle side borders

2 white strips 6" x 55" for middle top and bottom borders

2 red strips 4½" x 55" for outer side borders

2 red strips 4½" x 63" for outer top and bottom borders

Blocks:

5 white squares 15", trimmed to 14½" after the blocks are embroidered

Backing:

65" x 65"

Binding:

7 strips 2¼" x WOF

ASSEMBLY
Use a ¼" seam allowance for piecing.

❧ Refer to the Redwork instructions, page 15, and complete five blocks. Make two strip-sets with the following pieces: a 3¾" red strip, a 2½" white strip, and a 5¼" red strip. At a 45° angle, cut two side triangles from each of the strip-sets (Fig. 2–20).

❧ Refer to the quilt assembly diagram, page 62, to construct the center of the quilt. Trim the side and corner triangles to size, leaving a ¼" seam allowance, after adding them to the blocks.

❧ Sew the red inner side borders to the quilt, then the top and bottom borders, trimming each strip to size after stitching. Add the middle and outer borders to the quilt in the same manner.

❧ Refer to the pattern on page 63 and trace the border design onto the middle border and embroider.

❧ Layer the batting between the backing and quilt top. Quilt as desired, bind, and place a label on your quilt.

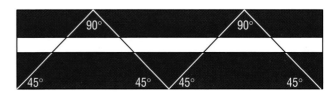

Fig. 2–20. Cut two side triangles at a 45° angle from each strip-set.

Quilt assembly.

Border redwork placement.

Pattern repeats at shaded leaves

REDWORK QUILT
full-size border pattern

TULIP TIME

Quilt size: 40" x 40"
Finished block size: 14"

Pattern 9, Tulip Circle, page 84, was used in this quilt
made by Vivian Miller, Columbus, Nebraska.

YARDAGE

Yardage is based on a 40"–45" WOF (width of fabric).

½ yard white fabric

½ yard light green fabric

⅝ yard medium green fabric

½ yard dark green fabric

½ yard purple fabric

½ yard green fabric for bias vines

44" x 44" batting

2⅝ yards backing

½ yard binding

CUTTING

Block:

1 light green square 16", trimmed to 14½" after the block is appliquéd

Framing:

2 dark green strips 2" x 14½" for sides

2 dark green strips 2" x 17½" for top and bottom

Corner triangles:

2 white squares 13½", cut in half diagonally

Borders:

2 purple strips 2½" x 24½" for inner side borders

2 purple strips 2½" x 28½" for inner top and bottom borders

2 medium green strips 4½" x 28½" for middle side borders

2 medium green strips 4½" x 36½" for middle top and bottom borders

2 dark green strips 2½" x 36½" for outer side borders

2 dark-green strips 2½" x 40½" for outer top and bottom borders

Backing:

44" x 44"

Binding:

5 strips 2¼" x WOF

ASSEMBLY

Use a ¼" seam allowance for piecing.

❖ Complete one block. Sew the framing strips to the sides of the block, then to the top and bottom. Sew the corner triangles to the edge of each framing strip, trimming to ¼" outside the point of the border (Fig. 2–21, page 66).

❖ Sew the inner borders to the sides of the quilt, then to the top and bottom. Sew the middle and outer borders to the quilt in the same manner.

❖ For bias vines, cut ¾" bias strips from the green fabric. Sew the strips together, end to end, to make one continuous strip at least 170" long. Fold the ¾" strip as shown in Fig. 1–2, page 10. Using gentle curves, arrange the vines on the borders and pin in place. Baste, then appliqué the stems on the border. Add flowers from the pattern chosen.

❖ Layer the batting between the backing and quilt top. Quilt as desired, bind, and place a label on your quilt.

Quilt assembly.

Fig. 2–21. Trim the triangles after piecing.

Border appliqué placement.

FLAME FLOWER

Quilt size: 31" x 31"
Finished block size: 14"

Pattern 8, Flame Flowers, page 83, was used in this quilt
made by Mary Weich, Norfolk, Nebraska.

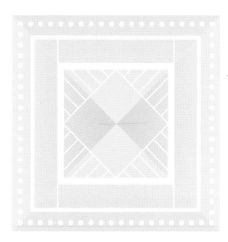

YARDAGE

Yardage is based on a 40"–45" WOF (width of fabric).

½ yard white fabric

¼ yard each of seven assorted fabrics

¼ yard fabric for inner border

¾ yard fabric for outer border

35" x 35" batting

1 yard backing

⅜ yard binding

CUTTING

Block:

1 white square 16", trimmed to 14½" after the block is appliquéd

Corner triangles:

4 strips 2½" x 10½" from each of the seven assorted fabrics

Borders:

2 strips 1½" x 20½" for inner side borders

2 strips 1½" x 22½" for inner top and bottom borders

2 strips 5" x 22½" for outer side borders

2 strips 5" x 31½" for outer top and bottom borders

Backing:

35" x 35"

Binding:

4 strips 2¼" x WOF

ASSEMBLY

Use a ¼" seam allowance for piecing.

❖ Complete one block. Join seven assorted strips to make a strip-set (Fig. 2–22). Make four of these strip-sets.

❖ Find the center of a strip-set and place it at the center of one side of the block. Sew a strip-set to the block. Sew another strip-set to the opposite side of the block. Trim the strip-sets at a 45° angle to form corner triangles, leaving a ¼" seam allowance as shown (Fig. 2–23, page 69).

❖ Repeat the previous step for the remaining two sides of the block.

❖ Before adding the inner borders, re-trim the edges of the quilt if necessary, leaving a ¼" seam allowance. Sew the inner side borders to the quilt, then the inner top and bottom borders, trimming the ends as necessary. Sew the outer borders to the quilt in the same manner.

❖ Layer the batting between the backing and quilt top. Quilt as desired, bind, and place a label on your quilt.

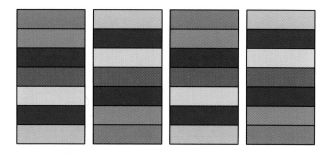

Fig. 2–22. Make four strip-sets.

Fig. 2–23. Trim the strip-set at a 45° angle, leaving a ¼" seam allowance.

Quilt assembly.

FLOWER ALBUM

Quilt size: 67" x 67"
Center finished block size: 18"
Outer finished block size: 14"

The following patterns were used in this quilt: 29, Crossed Peonies, page 104; 35, Rose Ring, page 110; 43, Poppy Ring, page 118; 32, Peony Ring, page 107; and the flower from 12, Wild Rose Circle, page 87, was placed on the ring pattern for the bottom right block. The Wild Rose was also used for the flowers on the setting triangles. The quilt was made by Gloria Miller, Columbus, Nebraska.

YARDAGE
Yardage is based on a 40"–45" WOF (width of fabric).

3 yards black fabric

1¼ yards medium pink fabric

1¾ yards dark pink fabric

71" x 71" batting

4 yards backing

⅝ yard binding

CUTTING
Cut black borders first, parallel to the selvage.

Borders:

8 black strips 2" x 53" for inner and
outer borders

8 medium pink strips 2½" x 40" for
middle borders

8 dark pink strips 2½" x 40" for middle borders

4 black squares 8½" for corners

Blocks:

1 black square 20", trimmed to 18½" after
the block is appliquéd

4 black squares 16", trimmed to 14½" after
the blocks are appliquéd

Center block triangles:

1 dark pink square 6¾", cut twice diagonally

Outer block framing:

8 medium pink strips 2½" x 14½"

8 medium pink strips 2½" x 18½"

Setting triangles:

4 dark pink strips 3¼" x 8" for
side triangles

4 black strips 6½" x 20" for side triangles

4 dark pink strips 4½" x 28" for side triangles

2 dark pink squares 14", cut twice diagonally,
for corner triangles

2 black squares 6", cut twice diagonally, for
corner triangles

Backing:

71" x 71"

Binding:

7 strips 2¼" x WOF

ASSEMBLY
Use a ¼" seam allowance for piecing.

❖ Complete five blocks. Refer to Fig. 2–24 and sew the dark pink center block triangles to the corners of the 18½" block, trimming the seam allowances to ¼".

Fig. 2–24. Sew the triangles to the corners of the center block diagonally and trim the seam allowances to ¼".

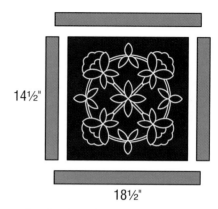

Fig. 2–25. Sew framing strips to each 14½" block.

Sew the framing strips to each 14½" block (Fig. 2–25). To construct the side setting triangles, you will need to assemble four strip-sets. Mark the centers of the following strips with a small "x": 8" dark pink, 20" black, and 28" dark pink. With right sides together, match the x's and sew the strips together. Cut a side triangle from each strip-set as shown in Fig. 2–26.

To construct the corner setting triangles, sew a black triangle to a pink triangle to make half of the corner (Fig. 2–27). Repeat for the remaining seven triangles. Trim the pink triangle to ¼" of the seam line. Sew the pieced triangles together to form the corner triangles (Fig. 2–28).

To assemble the middle border, refer to Fig. 2–29, page 73, and make four strip-sets. Cut 5½" segments from the strip-sets and sew seven segments together as shown in the quilt assembly diagram to form the border. Two strips will need to be trimmed from each border end.

Sew a 2" black strip to each side of the middle border. Sew two pieced borders to the sides of the quilt. Sew an 8½" black square to each end of the remaining two borders. Sew these borders to the top and bottom of the quilt.

Add appliqué to the side setting triangles. See page 74 for the pattern used in this quilt. Layer the batting between the backing and quilt top. Quilt as desired, bind, and place a label on your quilt.

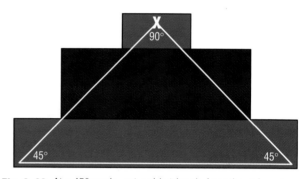

Fig. 2–26. At a 45° angle, cut a side triangle from the strip-set.

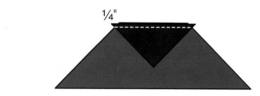

Fig. 2–27. Sew a black and pink triangle together to form half of the corner triangle.

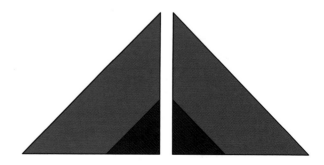

Fig. 2–28. Sew two pieced triangles to form a corner triangle.

5½"

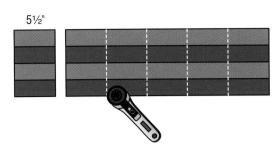

Fig. 2–29. Make four strip-sets for the middle border.

Quilt assembly.

FLOWER ALBUM
full-size side setting triangle
appliqué pattern

Pick-A-Pattern

This section contains 50 patterns. The patterns are interchangeable with the techniques and settings. Fabric requirements on each pattern page are for a single block. Refer to page 126 for instructions on making a full-size pattern from the quarter pattern presented.

SPRING TULIPS

Fabric required for one block:
- 16" square, trimmed to 14½"
- 12" x 14" stems and tulip bases
- 11" x 18" leaves
- 8" x 12" buds

IRIS

Fabric required for one block:
  16" square, trimmed to 14½"
  9" x 9" center
  8" x 10" center leaves
  11" x 11" iris top
  10" x 12" iris sides
  9" x 9" iris circle

3

SPINNING TULIPS 1

Fabric required for one block:

16" square, trimmed to 14½"
15" x 15" stems and leaves
6" x 6" tulip centers
8" x 8" tulip side petals
5" x 5" tulip bases
6" x 6" circles

SPINNING TULIPS 2

Fabric required for one block:

    16" square, trimmed to 14½"

    10" x 14" stems and leaves

    4" x 4" tulip tips

    4" x 11" tulips

4

5 SPINNING WILD ROSES

Fabric required for one block:

16" square, trimmed to 14½"
14" x 18" stems and leaves
10" x 10" roses
8" x 8" rose centers

PEONY CIRCLE

Fabric required for one block:

16" square, trimmed to 14½"
17" x 17" stems and leaves
6" x 13" peony centers
8" x 13" peony outer petals
6" x 11" peony bases

6

7 DAISY CIRCLE

Fabric required for one block:

16" square, trimmed to 14½"
17" x 17" stems and leaves
6" x 14" daisy middle petals
8" x 10" daisy center petals
15" x 15" daisy side petals
8" x 11" daisy bases

FLAME FLOWERS

Fabric required for one block:

- 16" square, trimmed to 14½"
- 3" x 3" center circle
- 5" x 5" second circle
- 7" x 7" third circle
- 9" x 9" fourth circle
- 14" x 17" outer bud
- 10" x 18" middle bud
- 9" x 12" center bud
- 8" x 10" leaves

8

9

TULIP CIRCLE

Fabric required for one block:

    16" square, trimmed to 14½"
    12" x 17" stems and leaves
    6" x 10" tulip tips
    12" x 17" tulips

COMPASS FLOWER

Fabric required for one block:
- 16" square, trimmed to 14½"
- 9" x 9" center circle
- 7" x 9" center leaves
- 12" x 14" stems and leaves
- 7" x 8" top flower buds
- 7" x 10" top flower bases
- 6" x 12" bottom flower buds
- 9" x 10" bottom flower bases

10

11

SWIRLING LEAVES

Fabric required for one block:
16" square, trimmed to 14½"
12" x 18" stems and leaves
9" x 9" end leaves

WILD ROSE CIRCLE

Fabric required for one block:

16" square, trimmed to 14½"
11" x 17" stems and leaves
12" x 13" flowers and buds
6" x 10" bud bases
6" x 6" flower centers

12

13 DOGWOOD CIRCLE

Fabric required for one block:

16" square, trimmed to 14½"
14" x 14" stems and leaves
12" x 18" flowers
8" x 9" flower centers
brown floss can be used for flower tips

POPPIES AND BUDS

Fabric required for one block:

16" square, trimmed to 14½"

12" x 17" stems, leaves, and bud bases

18" x 18" flowers

6" x 6" center circles

8" x 8" outer circles

15

LOOKS LIKE CHERRIES TO ME
Fabric required for one block:
  16" square, trimmed to 14½"
   8" x 12" center circle and leaves
  15" x 17" stems and leaves
  10" x 10" berries

PRETTY LEAVES
Fabric required for one block:
- 16" square, trimmed to 14½"
- 5" x 6" stems
- 14" x 16" leaves

17 ROSE AND BUDS

Fabric required for one block:

16" square, trimmed to 14½"

8" x 9" buds

15" x 16" stems, leaves, and bud bases

10" x 10" outer flower

8" x 8" middle flower

5" x 5" center flower

TULIP TIME 1

Fabric required for one block:

- 16" square, trimmed to 14½"
- 10" x 13" stems and leaves
- 9" x 12" flower tips
- 9" x 13" middle flowers
- 10" x 18" bottom flowers

18

19 TULIP TIME 2

Fabric required for one block:
- 16" square, trimmed to 14½"
- 14" x 17" stems and leaves
- 12" x 12" center circle
- 8" x 9" tulip tips
- 12" x 12" tulips

CROSSED CANDLE FLOWERS

Fabric required for one block:

    16" square, trimmed to 14½"
     6" x 6" center
     8" x 8" center circle
    13" x 13" stems, leaves, and flower bases
     8" x 8" buds
     7" x 9" small top petals
     8" x 12" large center petals
     8" x 9" small side petals
    10" x 14" large bottom petals

CROSSED ORCHIDS

21

Fabric required for one block:

16" square, trimmed to 14½"

6" x 6" center and 8" x 8" center circle

13" x 13" stems and leaves

8" x 8" buds

8" x 8" bottom petals

9" x 9" outer petals

9" x 9" middle petals

8" x 9" top center petals

6" x 6" orchid circles

CROSSED BUDS

Fabric required for one block:

16" square, trimmed to 14½"
6" x 6" center
8" x 8" center circle
14" x 17" leaves and stems
8" x 8" small buds
10" x 11" large center buds
6" x 15" large outer buds

23 CROSSED STAR FLOWERS

Fabric required for one block:

- 16" square, trimmed to 14½"
- 6" x 6" center
- 8" x 8" center circle
- 13" x 13" stems and leaves
- 8" x 8" small buds
- 15" x 15" flowers
- 9" x 11" inside flower petals
- 6" x 6" flower centers

CROSSED LOVE APPLES

Fabric required for one block:

16" square, trimmed to 14½"
6" x 6" center
8" x 8" center circle
12" x 12" leaves, stems, top and bottom of love apple
8" x 8" small buds
11" x 12" outer section of apples
9" x 12" middle section of apples
6" x 12" center section of apples

24

25 CROSSED LEAVES

Fabric required for one block:

16" square, trimmed to 14½"
6" x 6" center
8" x 8" center circle
15" x 15" stems and leaves
8" x 8" small buds
6" x 11" large buds

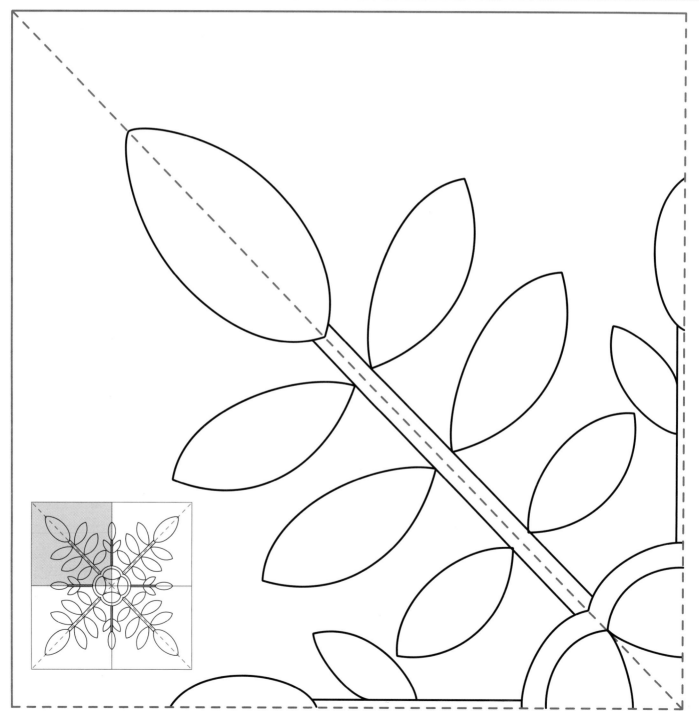

CROSSED FAN FLOWERS

Fabric required for one block:

16" square, trimmed to 14½"
6" x 6" center
8" x 8" center circle
12" x 14" stems, leaves, and flower bases
8" x 8" buds
14" x 15" outer flower petals
10" x 12" middle flower petals
7" x 10" flower centers

26

27 CROSSED ROSES

Fabric required for one block:

16" square, trimmed to 14½"
6" x 6" center
8" x 8" center circle
13" x 13" stems and leaves
8" x 8" small buds
13" x 13" flowers
6" x 10" crescents on flowers
9" x 10" flower petals

CROSSED WILD ROSES

Fabric required for one block:

- 16" square, trimmed to 14½"
- 6" x 6" center
- 8" x 8" center circle
- 13" x 15" stems and leaves
- 8" x 8" small buds
- 7" x 10" flower crowns
- 10" x 10" flowers
- 4" x 9" flower centers

28

29

CROSSED PEONIES

Fabric required for one block:

16" square, trimmed to 14½"
6" x 6" center
8" x 8" center circle
13" x 14" leaves and stems
8" x 8" small buds
8" x 14" outer petals
8" x 15" middle petals
8" x 10" flower centers
10" x 11" flower bases

CROSSED DOGWOODS

Fabric required for one block:

- 16" square, trimmed to 14½"
- 6" x 6" center
- 8" x 8" center circle
- 13" x 13" stems and leaves
- 8" x 8" small buds
- 15" x 15" flower petals
- 9" x 12" flower petal tips
- 8" x 8" flower centers

31 CROSSED FLOWERS

Fabric required for one block:

16" square, trimmed to 14½"

6" x 6" center and 8" x 8" center circle

13" x 13" stems and leaves

8" x 8" small buds

8" x 10" petals under center petal

12" x 12" center petals

10" x 10" first petals and 10" x 10" second petals

10" x 10" third petals

6" x 6" flower circles

PEONY RING

Fabric required for one block:

- 16" square, trimmed to 14½"
- 14" x 14" circle, stems, leaves, and bottom petals of flower
- 6" x 15" outer petals
- 7" x 15" middle petals
- 8" x 12" center petals
- 8" x 9" base petals
- 8" x 8" flower circles

33 LOVE APPLE RING

Fabric required for one block:

16" square, trimmed to 14½"

14" x 14" circle, stems, leaves, and top and bottom of apples

14" x 14" outer section of apples

9" x 15" middle section of apples

9" x 12" center section of apples

DOGWOOD RING

Fabric required for one block:

16" square, trimmed to 14½"
14" x 14" circle, stems, and leaves
9" x 10" flower petal tips
13" x 13" flower petals
6" x 6" flower circles

34

35

ROSE RING

Fabric required for one block:

    16" square, trimmed to 14½"
    14" x 14" circle, stems, and leaves
     9" x 10" center petals
    12" x 12" outer petals
    10" x 15" base petals

Tulip Ring

Fabric required for one block:
 16" square, trimmed to 14½"
 14" x 14" circle, stems, and leaves
 12" x 12" tulips
 10" x 10" tulip petals

37

CLEMATIS RING

Fabric required for one block:

16" square, trimmed to 14½"

14" x 14" circle, stems, and leaves

14" x 14" outer petals

12" x 12" inner petals

6" x 6" flower circles

SUNFLOWER RING

Fabric required for one block:

- 16" square, trimmed to 14½"
- 14" x 14" circle, stems, leaves, and flower bases
- 12" x 12" top petals
- 9" x 11" center petals
- 8" x 12" bottom petals

39 COCKSCOMB RING

Fabric required for one block:

16" square, trimmed to 14½"
14" x 14" circle, stems, and leaves
 6" x 8" top petals
10" x 14" center petals
10" x 14" bottom petals

114   *Pick-A-Pattern* APPLIQUÉ & VARIATIONS – *Joan Waldman*

CANDLE FLOWER RING

Fabric required for one block:

16" square, trimmed to 14½"
14" x 14" circle, stems, leaves, and flower bases
8" x 15" top petals
10" x 11" flower centers
9" x 11" bottom petals

41 CONE FLOWER RING

Fabric required for one block:

16" square, trimmed to 14½"

14" x 14" circle, stems, and leaves

11" x 12" outer flower petals

10" x 10" second flower petals

7" x 11" center flower petals

10" x 15" lower flower petals

Pick-A-Pattern APPLIQUÉ & VARIATIONS – *Joan Waldman*

GRAPE RING

Fabric required for one block:
16" square, trimmed to 14½"
14" x 14" circle, stems, and leaves
10" x 18" grapes

43 POPPY RING

Fabric required for one block:

    16" square, trimmed to 14½"

    14" x 14" circle, stems, leaves, and flower bases

    10" x 14" center petals

    10" x 15" side petals

    9" x 12" bottom petals

SPRINGTIME

Fabric required for one block:

- 16" square, trimmed to 14½"
- 12" x 14" stems, leaves, and bud bases
- 15" x 15" flowers and buds
- 5" x 8" flower centers

45

MORNING GLORIES
Fabric required for one block:

16" square, trimmed to 14½"

11" x 12" stems and leaves, and flower bases

10" x 12" top of flowers

4" x 11" bottom of flowers

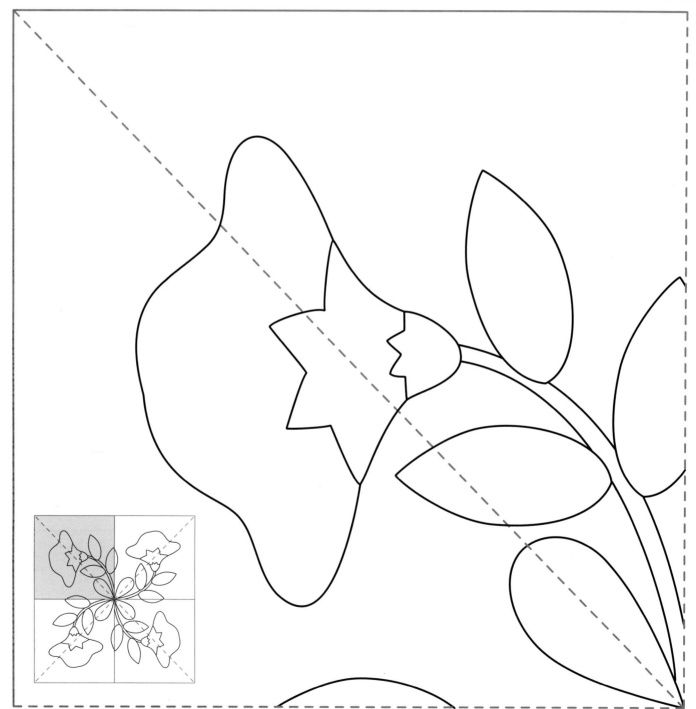

COSMOS

Fabric required for one block:

- 16" square, trimmed to 14½"
- 12" x 14" stems and leaves
- 12" x 14" flowers
- 3" x 5" outer circle
- 3" x 5" inner circle
- 2" x 2" center of leaves

46

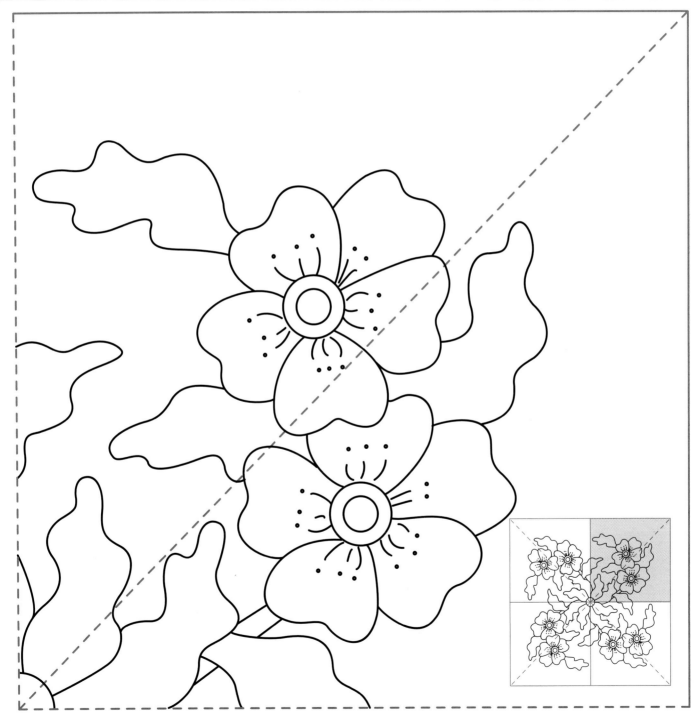

47 ROSES

Fabric required for one block:

16" square, trimmed to 14½"

7" x 7" center stems

8" x 10" stems and leaves

10" x 12" outer section of roses

9" x 9" inner section of roses

5" x 5" buds and center of roses

GAILLARDIA

Fabric required for one block:

16" square, trimmed to 14½"
11" x 14" stems and leaves
14" x 14" flowers
6" x 6" flower centers
embroidery floss for jagged lines

49 NASTURTIUMS

Fabric required for one block:
16" square, trimmed to 14½"
10" x 10" stems and leaves
10" x 10" flowers and buds

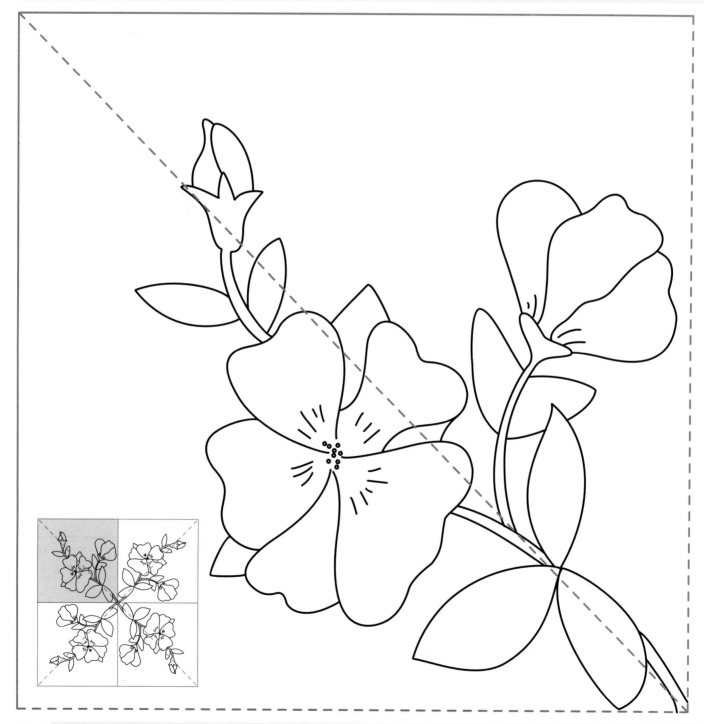

POINSETTIA

Fabric required for one block:

16" square, trimmed to 14½"
12" x 12" stems and leaves
14" x 14" flowers and buds
 6" x 6" centers

50

Making a Full-Size Pattern

All patterns show a quarter of the block. To make a complete pattern, fold a 14" square of tracing paper in half, and then in half again to form four quadrants. Open the tracing paper and place one quadrant over the pattern, aligning the dashed lines on the pattern with the fold lines on the tracing paper. Trace the pattern with a heavy, permanent marker (Fig. 3–1). Fold the tracing paper in half, right side out, and copy the pattern from the first quadrant to the opposite quadrant of the tracing paper (Fig. 3–2). Unfold, then fold the paper in half in the opposite direction and copy the traced pattern onto the remaining quadrants (Fig. 3–3).

Fig. 3–2. Fold the paper in half and trace the pattern to the opposite side.

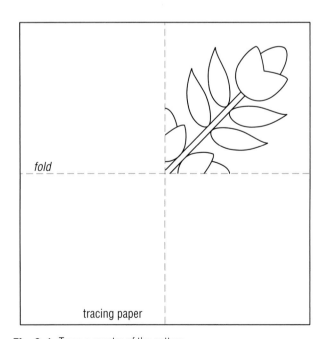

Fig. 3–1. Trace a quarter of the pattern.

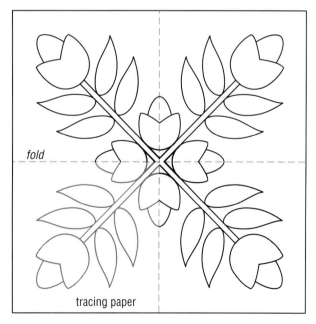

Fig. 3–3. Copy the pattern onto the remaining quadrants.

Finishing Your Quilt

Borders

In the Pick-A-Settings section, some of the settings have borders that contain vines and flowers from the designs in the blocks, and a diagram for appliqué placement on the borders is presented with those settings. If you choose a different block from the one pictured in the setting section, the flowers and leaves from your choice may be used in the border.

For example, in the SPINNING TULIPS quilt, the tulips in the border vine can be replaced with irises. If you are not sure how this will look, trace the flowers on paper, cut them out, and place them on the border. Occasionally, a few more flowers, leaves, or buds may need to be added to balance the design.

DESIGNING YOUR OWN BORDER

1 Measure the length and width of the quilt top. Mark these measurements on a roll of draftsman's tracing or freezer paper, then cut the paper to the size marked.

2 For vine placement guides, fold the paper in half lengthwise, and then in half again (Fig. 4–1). You may make another fold to divide the border into eight equal increments for tighter curves in your design.

3 Sketch a vine on one section of the border. A draftsman's flexible curve is a helpful tool for this. The vine can be copied to the rest of the border by folding the paper and tracing the vine onto the next section.

4 Add flowers and leaves from your chosen pattern by tracing them on the vines. Add more leaves as needed to make the vine visually pleasing (Fig. 4–2, page 129).

5 Continue the vine around the corners of the quilt in a "U" shape. Again, add flowers and leaves as desired (Fig. 4–3, page 129).

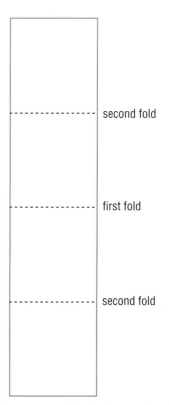

second fold

first fold

second fold

Fig. 4–1. Fold the paper in half lengthwise, and then in half again.

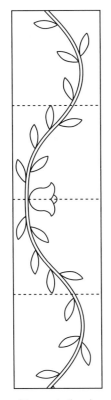

Fig. 4–2. Add flowers and leaves to the vine.

Fig. 4–3. Draw a "U" in the corner of the borders and add flowers and leaves as desired.

Machine Quilting

Machine quilting is a quick way to finish your projects. On your sewing machine, you will need a walking foot for straight-line quilting and a darning or embroidery foot for free-form quilting. To do free-form quilting, drop or cover your feed dogs. Your machine manual should tell you how to accomplish this.

For machine quilting, I use #70/10, #80/12, or #90/14 regular sewing needles. If you plan to use metallic thread, there is a special metallic needle available at most fabric shops. The thread you choose is a personal decision. Try different brands and types until you find the one you like. You can also use invisible monofilament thread as the top thread. This thread is available in clear for light fabrics and smoke for dark fabrics. My preference for bobbin thread is lingerie and bobbin thread. These come in black and white. A good-quality thread makes the quilting process easier.

PREPARING THE QUILT

1 Lay the backing on a flat surface. Two or more large tables pushed together or a clean floor works well. Tape the backing, wrong side up, to the surface with masking tape.

2 Smooth the batting on top of the backing and tape in place. Smooth the quilt top over the batting, right side up, and tape in place.

3 Pin through all layers with 1" craft pins or curved 1" safety pins, available in quilt and craft stores. Place a pin approximately every 4" throughout the quilt. Try to pin where you will not be quilting.

4 When the pinning is complete, trim the batting to within ½" of the quilt top. Bring the backing over the batting and pin it to the quilt top. This keeps the batting from being torn during the quilting process.

STRAIGHT-LINE QUILTING

1 Roll the quilt from one edge until you reach the middle. On your machine, attach the walking foot and thread the top and bobbin with your desired threads.

2 Stitch in the ditch (in the seamline) on all block lines, vertical and horizontal. Reroll the quilt as necessary. Quilt the seams in the borders, if any.

3 Mark the quilting designs on plain blocks and on any areas where you plan to add quilting. For marking, I use a silver quilter's pencil. Keep the pencil sharp and mark lightly. Quilt an area directly after marking. Most of the markings will have disappeared by the time you finish quilting. The remaining markings will come out when the quilt is laundered for the first time.

FREE-MOTION QUILTING

Free-motion quilting can be done more easily if your machine is turned so the head faces you (Fig. 4–4, page 131). If you have a free-arm machine, put the extension tray in place. Raising the back of the machine is also helpful. This can be done by placing a 4"–5" rubber door stop under each edge of the back of the machine (Fig. 4–5, page 131).

1 Drop the feed dogs and put the darning foot on the machine.

2 Slip the quilt under the needle and begin quilting at the center of the quilt. Quilt one block or area at a time. This may seem awkward at first, but it makes moving the quilt under the needle easier.

3 Quilt from the center out toward the borders. When finished, trim all three layers even with the edge of the quilt top. Now the quilt is ready for binding.

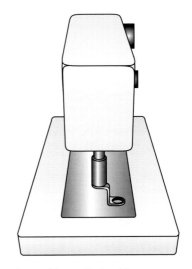

Fig. 4–4. Turn the machine so the head faces you.

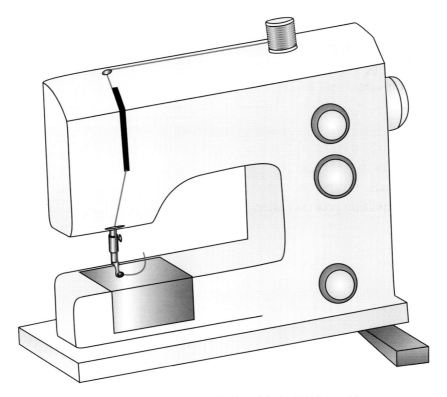

Fig. 4–5. Place a rubber door stop under each edge of the back of the machine.

Binding

Follow these steps to make a ¼" double binding around your quilt.

1. Cut 2¼" strips selvage to selvage across the binding fabric. Cut enough strips to equal the length around your quilt, plus about 10". Trim selvages off the strips.

2. Lay two strips, right sides together, at a 90° angle and overlap the strip ends approximately ¼". Stitch across the two strips diagonally. Continue sewing the strips together until they are all joined. Trim the seam allowance to ¼" (Fig. 4–6).

3. Press the binding in half lengthwise, wrong sides together. Press the seams that join the strips open as you come to them.

4. Before sewing the binding to the quilt, pin one end of the binding to the quilt along a side. Pull the binding around the quilt and make sure that a seam in the binding does not fall on the corners of the quilt. If it does, adjust the starting place until each corner is without a seam.

5. Leaving about 10" of binding free, align the raw edge of the binding to the raw edge of the quilt. Sew the folded binding to the quilt (Fig. 4–7).

6. Sew the first side of the quilt until you are ¼" from the end. Backstitch. Lift the presser foot and turn the quilt. Fold the binding straight up at the corner, then fold it down, aligning the raw edge of the binding with the raw edge of the quilt (Fig. 4–8). This makes a small miter at the corner. Begin sewing the second side of quilt ¼" from the edge. Continue sewing around the quilt in the same manner.

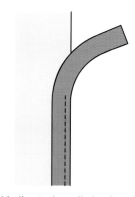

Fig. 4–7. Sew the binding to the quilt, leaving about 10" unstitched.

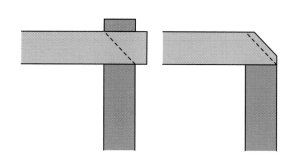

Fig. 4-6. Sew a diagonal seam. Trim, leaving a ¼" seam allowance.

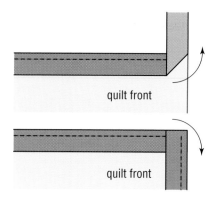

quilt front

quilt front

Fig. 4–8. Fold the binding up at the corner, then down to align with the quilt edge.

7 To join the binding, stop sewing approximately 10" from the beginning stitch. Backstitch. Lay the two ends of binding so they overlap.

8 Cut about a 2" piece off the end of the binding. Unfold this piece and lay it on top, perpendicular to the overlapped bindings. Trim the binding ends so that ¼" of the binding is on either side of the unfolded piece (Fig. 4–9).

9 Unfold the binding ends and place right sides together with ¼" overlapping on both edges. Sew a diagonal seam and trim the excess fabric (Fig. 4–10).

10 Finger press the diagonal seam open, refold the binding, and finish sewing it in place. Turn the binding to the back of the quilt and hand stitch in place (Fig. 4–11).

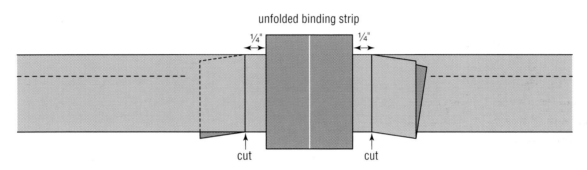

Fig. 4–9. Use an unfolded piece of binding as a guide to trim the ends ¼" away from the edge of the guide.

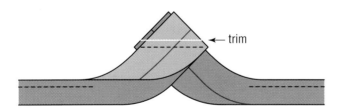

Fig. 4–10. Sew a diagonal seam and trim the excess fabric.

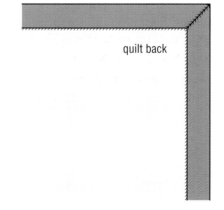

Fig. 4–11. Use a blind stitch to sew the binding to the back of the quilt.

About the Author

Joan Waldman grew up on a farm near Humphrey, Nebraska. Since the mid-1970s, she has been a quiltmaker, designer, and teacher.

For years, Joan sketched pieced designs and settings on graph paper and eventually began to draw appliqué designs. This was mostly done in the evenings, after her children were in bed. As her children grew up and left the nest, Joan began stitching the designs that had lived only on paper for so long.

With numerous sketch books full of design ideas, one of Joan's greatest joys is sharing her designs with others. She is continually searching for new ways to create with fabric and thread. Providing her designs with a variety of techniques and settings is Joan's forte.

She is co-founder of the Calico Quilt Club of Columbus, Nebraska, and member of the Country Piecemakers Quilt Guild of Norfolk, Nebraska, Nebraska State Quilt Guild, NQA, and AQS.

Other AQS Books

This is only a small selection of the books available from the American Quilter's Society. AQS books are known worldwide for timely topics, clear writing, beautiful color photos, and accurate illustrations and patterns. The following books are available from your local bookseller, quilt shop, or public library.

#6001   us$21.95

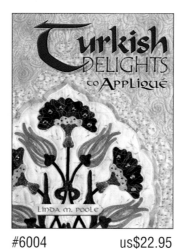

#6004   us$22.95

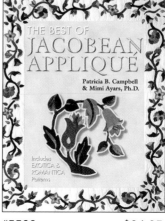

#5588   us$24.95

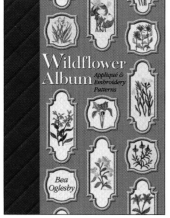

#5757   us$19.95

#6211   us$19.95

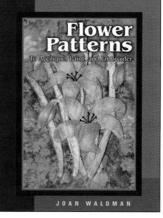

#5238   us$19.95

#5855   us$22.95

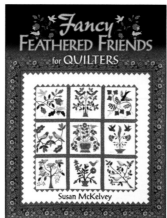

#6205   us$24.95

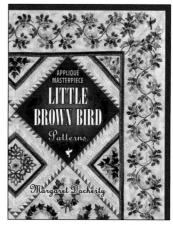

#5338   us$21.95

Look for these books nationally or call 1-800-626-5420